The dynamics of community

Sister Marie Beha O. S. F.

The dynamics of community

CORPUS BOOKS

New York / Cleveland

CORPUS PUBLICATIONS

editorial offices
110 East 59th Street
New York, New York 10022

sales & distribution
2231 West 110th Street
Cleveland, Ohio 44102

Library of Congress Catalog Card Number: 72-135450
PRINTED IN THE UNITED STATES OF AMERICA

Contents

The dynamics of community

Introduction

WRITING A BOOK these days is, in a sense, inexcusable boldness. Times change, and at present they are changing so fast that the gap between typewriter and printing press, between what is being written and what is being read is almost unbridgeable. In addition to this time differential, any writer today must live in fear that times will change his own mind and that he will then have to live with the obligation to explain away what he once held to be true.

Given all these reasons for not writing a book, what would be a possible justification. I can only offer a kind of "justification by faith." I happen to believe in community, to believe in it enough to want to work through and to live with its dynamics. And for me such belief must be given expression in a specific profession of faith-made-public. This profession is also something of a confession, an open admission of what is yet incomplete and needs to be worked out in my own life and in the life and thought of others.

So *The Dynamics of community* is intended to be a credo. It is also meant to be a tribute to all those both in the community of my own religious congregation and in the wider community of all my friends whose support and understanding have made community possible for me. I am particularly grateful to Father William Yeomans, SJ and to Dr. William May who have worked with this book editorially, to the superior general of my religious congregation, Sister M. Francine Zeller, OSF, and to my parents, Mr. and Mrs. H. F. Beha. Finally I am grateful to the community of Sisters with whom I have lived and worked this year, Sister Mary Evangeline McSloy RSM, Sister M. Claudia Zeller OSF, and Sister Veronica of Mary Magee SNJM; by the dynamics of their lives these Sisters have helped me to grow toward more realistic community.

1 / Formation in and for community

*It is extremely important to recall the importance
of the role played in formation by the atmosphere
of generosity provided by a fervent and united
community, in the midst of which young religious
will be enabled to learn by experience the value of
mutual fraternal assistance as an element of readier
progress and perseverance in their vocation.*
On Renewal of Religious Formation, Feb. 1, 1969, par. 5

THE CAPACITY to live in community has always been one of the
criteria for successful adaptation to religious life. But in the past it
was only one of many elements in religious formation. Living under
rule, submissiveness to superiors, capacity for poverty, for celibacy,
for sustaining routine: these have been central elements forming
generations of religious whose devotion to duty and disciplined lives
have played a key role in the growth of the American church.

But today's religious must form themselves in another way, or
risk not being formed at all. Formation through careful submission
to a detailed rule is no longer possible. The details are gone and
emphasis has shifted to personal responsibility and free decision.
Submission to superiors no longer calls for the ritual of multiple
permissions; poverty, celibacy, work—all demand more creativity,
more discovery of responses that are appropriate in the here and
now. These responses must be meaningful for the individual; they
must also be formed in and through community.

Forming community, then, assumes a central position in religious
life, both for those who are entering religious congregations, as

well as for those whose life-commitment must be constantly actualized in the day to day situation in which they find themselves. That such formation does take place in community is the fundamental belief behind an individual's choice of commitment to Christ within the context of a particular kind of community. It is also the daily experience of all whose lives are really lived in response to the demands of community. It is the hope of this book to explore some of the various forms of community and then to concentrate on the formation of truly Christian communities. Out of such a description of Christian community comes an understanding of the incarnational and paschal aspects which mark a community with the sign of God's presence.

A human community is always an incarnate community in which spirit is embodied and expressed in structures that give it a certain form and shape. Since every community is made up of many different individuals, its incarnational reality is also expressed pluralistically. And this, not in some once and for all form, but in the dynamism of constant growth and development. Finally, the incarnational aspect of Christian community expresses its spirit of out-going service in some concrete forms, some specific tasks.

Just as structure, pluralism, change, and task incarnate the Christian community, so too, suffering, asceticism and the tension of temptation mark a community with its cross and sign it as being redeemed. But for the Christian community, as for the baptized individual, these diminishments are not the end but only a passing on to fuller life and hoped for resurrection. The Christian community experiences some of this new life in the strength and support of communal faith, in the joy and peace of shared prayer. Here, especially, the fruits of living together in community give promise of the unity that will someday be realized in the communion of saints.

The dynamics by which Christians are formed and form themselves in and through community are the subject of special attention and study in the present period of religious history. This is the result of the renewed understanding that the church has of itself, as people called to be a community, and of the development of a better understanding of what it means to live in community. In the past, it seems that successful adjustment to community included such items as ability to get along with people, without becoming too "attached" to any of them; capacity to adjust to many different people within a relatively short space of time; a spirit of kindness and helpful service with emphasis on doing things for others. Today, formation for community would be more likely to stress capacity to form warm personal relationships; ability to move from a small, personally close core group to ever widening circles of community; sensitivity to others and their need of love and understanding; capacity for self-gift; ability to dialogue with others.

All this points to the centrality of community for all formation: for those entering the religious congregation who must form themselves for community, and all the members of a congregation who must constantly accept the responsibility of forming community and being formed themselves within community and through communication. Such is the daily conversion of heart called for by the Spirit, speaking through the very real demands of close, interpersonal relationships.

Formation for community

Formation for community must be formation in and by community. It cannot be accomplished by well-constructed lectures on "How to live community." The "How to live" can only come through living. Practice is so important in this area that theory can only be meaningful in terms of what has already been experienced. Reflection that follows after experience is real; reflection that precedes experience risks the selfishness of dreams.

If formation through community can be accepted as basic, it would seem to follow that experience of community as it is really lived in a particular congregation would be essential to the formation of any aspirant for religious life. By this is meant not the carefully controlled, homogeneous grouping of novitiate or postulate but the fallible, pluralistic life-style of the community, experienced in local houses and small apostolic groups. This is not to say that aspirants to community no longer need any introduction to community. It is simply to suggest that growth in community living can only come from practice, accompanied by personal direction and followed by opportunities for synthesis. A formation program like this puts tremendous demands on the local group to live in community, to be so skilled themselves that their very lives express community. While programs of formation can be generalized and to some extent made secure, formation of individuals, within individual communities, has to remain open and flexible. Discernment of spirits, that gift for discovering the needs and talents of the candidate and the corresponding needs and strengths of the local community, will be a prime requisite for religious superiors.

Formation for community will also give increasing consideration to the unique spirit of the local house. Just as the people who form community are different, so to, each local community is individual and hence uniquely formative. A suitable candidate for a particular congregation could be described as one who is responsive to this community's formative influence. He is able to form community with the members of a particular local group. On the other hand, if a person is unable to be formed by the community and to form community with this unique group, then he is not a suitable candidate, or at least, not suitable for this particular community.

Such a formation in community should help the candidate to come to grips, right from the beginning of religious life, with the demands and the rewards of living in community. In a real, lived situation his vocation could be tested with such realism that the decision either to commit himself for life in celibate community or to give himself in a family community could be based on personal experience and comparison of the two life-styles. Hopefully this decision could be less painful because it is more evident, and more enduring because it is more real.

Formation programs should place new emphasis on the essential discipline of religious life, which is the capacity for living in close interpersonal contact, outside the natural supportive structure of a family; in short, they must stress the capacity for celibate community. Such an emphasis could prevent religious from rudely awakening, later in life, to the fact that they entered a congregation but were never prepared to live in a community.

Formation for community, within community, should also help to break down the artificial distinction between those in formation and the professed religious. To live is to grow and develop always. To continue in community is to be always in formation, shaped by all those with whom one lives. So the suggestions that follow on how community forms its members and on the need for openness to these formative influences are applicable to all who make the choice to live in community.

Formation through forming community

In a sense, to talk about how community forms its members is also to discuss how the members form community. If a community is not constantly being formed, there is no real community, its dynamism is gone; it is sick, perhaps dying, and so can only infect and weaken its members. But if community is being formed in a particular, here and now situation, then the members are being formed, first of all, by their very effort to live together in community.

This being with and for each other is the realism of community and, consequently, its force for growth and development. But this presupposes that community is more than polite, surface exchange. Just as interpersonal relationships, or the binding together of persons in truth and love, is what forms community, so only this kind of living together releases the potential of formation in and through community.

This implies that formation in community presupposes a group that wants to form a community, to meet other persons "not where the mind, but where the heart decides," to borrow the phrasing of Teilhard. The mind plans, generalizes, and aims for the objective, but the heart knows only the individual, the personal and so accepts what is beyond all calculation. Consequently, formation in community cannot be predetermined, scheduled. It happens where and when community happens. And it *will* happen, if the persons involved are willing and open; willing, for example, to lay aside the role playing and emphasis on position that safeguards persons from really relating, as persons, to each other. It implies valuation in terms of one's contribution to community and this on a scale that bears very little relation to position outside the personal community. Above all, formation in community must be based on a desire not only to be formed but also to be formed in this particular way. Every man desires, at least in theory, the growth potential of constant formation, but he may not feel called to be formed in a close, personal, celibate community.

One reason a person may not be able to accept the formative influences of community is his impatience with this slow, organic form of growth. He may still be looking for a short cut to individual perfection or at least for a way that risks less personal involvement. Past experiences or present fears may have left him so suspicious of interpersonal relationships that he will unconsciously resist the formative influence of the community. Such a person must first make his peace with these fears; otherwise he will never form community, nor be formed by it.

In contrast, one of the signs of a realistic desire to live in community is willingness to set aside one's preconceived notions of perfection and instant community in order to accept others in patience. For unless the members of a community know that their mistakes will be accepted because they, as persons, are accepted, they will not risk revealing themselves, and the strain of trying to be perfect will contradict any possibility of being truly human. Patience with mistakes implies being patient with oneself. Just as an impatient person begins by blaming himself but ends by blaming everyone else, so the patient man begins by accepting himself as a mistake-maker and so grows in toleration of all his fellow humans. Part of patience with self is the admission that one has made, and will make, mistakes. Mistakes admitted call for forgiveness; mistakes concealed and covered over, like all lies, call for still more dishonesty that disrupts community.

One of the criteria of a person's adjustment to life in community is this willingness to admit his own mistakes, joined to a willingness to live with the mistakes of others. These mistakes too, need to be admitted and not covered over with a layer of polite, thinly veiled condemnation. Perhaps the golden rule here could be "not to say unto others, what one would not say first to the person himself."

Another way in which community is formative centers around increasing sensitivity to the needs of the community and realism as to how each member can contribute to these needs. Every person in community is constantly being formed in response to the needs of his fellow man. He grows in a capacity for sympathy, when he responds to the suffering of others. He grows in ability to love, when others reveal less lovable aspects of themselves, and he is able to penetrate beneath their difficulties and discover the hurt, frightened person underneath. The very uniqueness of persons presents a tremendous range of ever-changing needs. Ability to respond implies the capacity for perceiving these needs as they are revealed here and now.

The needs of persons in community range from deep personal needs of acceptance, affection, and love to very pragmatic needs for advice and a helping hand. To substitute sympathy for shared doing of a job can be as completely unrealistic as to defend oneself from close personal relationships by a busy sort of serving: both are failures in community. The other side of this same coin is willingness to let one's own needs be known, to accept the support and help of others. It almost seems that this latter point is more critical, more authentic as a criterion, than the former. The person who is always willing to give help but is never willing to accept it may only be looking for one more opportunity for self-aggrandizement; he seems lacking in the essential community virtue of gratitude.

But to be sensitive to the needs of others, to be willing to reveal one's own needs and to accept the help of the community, is only part of forming and being formed by community. Another part is an appreciation of what the person can contribute to meet these needs. Here is an area where community members are in particular need of meeting each other in truth and love. Only with and through each other can the needs of a community, as well as the needs of individual members, be determined and then met realistically.

Community can also help its members to grow in sensitivity to needs outside of its own immediate circle. Each member of a community, just because he is a unique person, will see needs that no one else sees. Past training and present opportunity will allow each person to bring a sense of wider community to his own immediate community. Each person will also bring certain skills and insights for practical implementation that will help a community to realize its desire to serve.

A community that is going to retain its dynamism must be committed to real response to today's real needs, which are as all-embracing as the community of man itself. Here again members of a community need each other not only to attempt to do something about world problems but even to support the growing realization of the extent and complexity of these concerns. Just as the depth of need disclosed by one other suffering individual can be overwhelming, so too a man, left to himself with his vision of what the world, the church, his country need, can come close to despair.

Formation through communication

One of the skills most needed in community is a capacity for communication. Formation in community should provide for growth in this area while inability to communicate should be recognized as a breakdown in community itself or in the individual's ability to share. So much has been written on communication skills that any attempt to summarize here would be worse than inadequate. Let it suffice to show again some of the links between communication and community.

For one thing, communication is based on an ability to leave behind one's own preoccupations and prejudices, to enter somehow into the world of another person. To communicate with another is to try to understand him and to show this understanding in words, in gestures, in any way that seems appropriate. This kind of personal communication, which is formative of personal community, does not correspond directly to opportunities for conversation. In fact, a great deal of talk can be protection from communication and hide a real inability to communicate.

In community, it seems important that communication occur not only between individuals, as individuals, but also within the community as a whole. It is quite possible for individuals to be able to communicate with other individuals and still not be able to communicate as a group. How to develop community communication is a question that needs much research and experimentation. Certainly "group discussion" will not automatically ensure communication and may even serve as an excuse from an obligation to go beneath the surface of information exchange. On the other hand, opportunities for the group to interact as a group are basic to formation in community. It will certainly take time for the members of a community to grow in openness to communicate with each other. Before any real communication takes place, individuals forming community must begin to trust each other. This is a slow process even on the one-to-one level; it can be expected to be even slower on the level of a community.

One of the signs of such a growing trust is the ability to disagree. As someone experienced in group processes has pointed out, communities seem to go through a three-stage process. First of all, there is the honeymoon stage, when everyone in the group gets along beautifully with all the others. Like most honeymoons this is a relatively short period. It is followed by a more extended stage when members find themselves in increasing disagreement. This is the period when communication becomes most painful. The easy solution seems to be to stay apart, to say as little as possible, to avoid difficult topics. So misunderstanding compounds. What begins as an attempt to prevent hard feelings, creates a climate of distrust.

This is not to suggest that every truth one sees, or thinks one sees, should be aired on every occasion. To speak the truth in love is the Pauline ideal. Concretely, the dilemma whether to speak or to be silent in a particular situation can be crystallized by asking: Why would I speak? Why would I be silent? If my honest response is one of concern for the other, then I have come to a practical conclusion. Specifically, in terms of dissent, if I am silent to save myself trouble, to secure the good opinion of others, then my silence is selfish. I have failed to form the community, and I have also prevented the community from forming me: from correcting me, if my opinion is wrong; from accepting my trust, if my opinion is correct.

Only when the members of a community are willing to risk the pain of disagreement can they emerge from stage two and finally come to the joys of consensus in stage three. Today a great deal is being written about consensus emerging from community and also about forming community in the dynamics of its own evolution. In consensus, each individual member's opinion is respected; everyone speaks; everyone listens. The resulting consensus is not a compromise formed by somehow splicing all or most of the variant opinions together. Rather it is a new position, created by true communication. In the process of the give and take that results in true consensus, community is formed. Without such a consensus, community will not endure.

When a community is being formed, when an individual is being formed in community, one can expect to pass through unmitigated joy to painful disagreement and finally arrive at a form of consensus that is some indication of the level of community in a congregation. This level of community and communication will provide one of the strongest formative influences, both for those entering the congregation and for those who are being formed in and through forming community.

Such a formation in community has little of the stigma that is sometimes attached to the word *formation* with its connotation of being passively shaped by the influence of other persons and of one's environment. Such passivity would be more realistically termed *de-formation,* since it certainly would be destructive of person. In contrast, formation through forming community is true response, that is, responsible, personal action.

2 / Forms of community

*The communities that will count in the future will
arise between people who understand each other
and whose presence, even at a distance, makes a
profound difference in each other's lives.*

EUGENE KENNEDY, *Fashion Me A People**

SINCE VATICAN II an endless procession of books and articles has
appeared on community, but there remains a fundamental ambiguity
about the term. Is community first of all a physical reality? "He
entered the community." Or is it an expression of psychological
union? "We really experienced community at that liturgy." Or
is it a goal-oriented term? "We believe in the community of
saints." Is community a possibility or only a dream? Can community
be built or is it something that happens? Is the heart of community the interpersonal relationships of the members with the
consequence that community has an element of inwardness? Or
is it support and strength for the apostolate, in which case community is essentially turned out to others?

Origin of Community

It seems to be generally accepted that community is not a luxury,
added to man's way of life—it is his way of life; it is his becoming

*(New York: Sheed and Ward, 1967), p. 151.

a person. Max Scheler, a German phenomenologist of the early twentieth century, says this even more strongly. For him, man is not only made for communion with other men, he also begins his life experience with the notion of *we* and only gradually comes to some understanding of the *I*.[1] A very small child, for instance, is globally aware of the world around him and only gradually comes to an awareness of the world of the *me* and the *non-me*. As he matures, he learns more and more about a world that not only is *non-me* but bears very little relationship to the *me*. In other words, the world of *non-me* is seen more realistically as the world of *the other*.

Through the other, the maturing person comes to know more and more of himself, as a distinct being, different from the other, gifted in his own right. At times this revelation of self through the other will take on an element of the negative: I am not. At other times, the affirmation of "I am" will predominate. In either case self-awareness is a lifelong process involving a dynamic balance of positive and negative elements. According to Scheler, not only does man begin his growth from the solid foundation of the *we*, but he has such a basic, built-in notion of community that even if he were totally lacking in experience of others, man would still be ordered to community. Concretely, a Robinson Crusoe awakening as an adult on his island, without any experience of community, would still know loneliness, would still be unfulfilled in his acts of loving and sympathizing.[2]

In a very real way, a person who is deprived of love and understanding, who is given few opportunities to relate to others, is seriously handicapped as a person. If this deprivation comes early in his life, his whole growth will be stunted; if it comes later in life, he may be crippled and misshapen. And to some extent every man is handicapped by his own selfishness and by the selfishness of others. Such is man's original sin, the crack from which so many other flaws originate.

One final aspect of Scheler's phenomenology of community can provide basic insights into the levels of community and the bond of personal community. Scheler speaks of four forms of social unity. The lowest is the herd, or the mass. Here the bond that unites the members of the community is emotional, impulsive. Though the community or the mob lacks moral solidarity, it does have legal responsibility. The force of strong emotional ties makes the mass a powerful and dangerous form of social grouping. Its instinctive character gives it a kind of appeal and allows for release of pent-up emotion.

A second form of social unity is the life community, for example, the family, the tribe, the nation. Such a community is spontaneous and unplanned; the members are held together by something so much a part of their lives that this bond can never be dissolved, even if it is denied. Moreover a life community is a value in itself; it makes its own values, and these determine the life-style of the members.

A third form of social unity is that of the society, where the unity of the members is artificial and planned, in contrast to the natural, spontaneous unity of the family. The bond of unity is less than personal and may be summarized in terms of such utilitarian goals as usefulness, efficiency of action, pleasure. Because society is an artificially designed structure, it is highly rule-oriented. Each society makes its own rules and is governed by these self-designed regulations. Accepting membership in a society implies acceptance of its rules though this acceptance may be conditioned and include a desire to change the rules. In short, the members of a society enter into a contractual and hence limited relationship with each other.

The fourth form of social unity is that of the person community. Scheler characterizes this community as one in which the members are united by solidarity of salvation and in which the bond is one of love. In a person community each of the members is *coresponsible,* not only for the other members of the group, but also for the group as a whole.

Reflections on levels of community

Scheler's description of the levels of community calls attention to the fact that communiy is an analogous term. It has many meanings, and although these meanings have certain common elements, critical differences within these meanings make it imperative for us to distinguish various levels of community. A community is always a union of persons; the bond of community is more than mere physical juxtaposition; it is both affective and effective. The exact nature of this bond is what seems to differentiate communities, distinguishing one level from the other. But not only is community an analogous term; its reality is also experienced as complementary levels in the lives of persons who form community. Man needs social unity in all these various forms and his existence is truncated if he lacks experience at any one level.

Concretely, man needs to experience the anonymity and emotional release of the mass. He needs to feel that he belongs to something bigger than he is, to feel that he is part of some group. Instinctively people seek to re-create themselves by setting aside some of their more pressing responsibilities and participating in some activity that makes only limited demands upon them. A *mass* of persons attends a football game and is caught up for the moment in the limited responses called for by "first down, goal to go," and "tied in the fourth quarter." Similarly, a person who plays on the team or takes part in some group effort can both lose himself and find himself. Nor is the constructive release of the mass confined to "games people play." Any form of social unity that is characterized by a bond that is predominately emotional and instinctive allows men to satisfy this basic need for the community of the mass. Doing simple tasks together, providing opportunities for a group to enjoy each other's company, crying together, laughing together—all these are community exercises.

On the level of the life community, every man belongs to several concentric circles of community: his family community, his racial community, his national community, the human community. Since all of these forms of social unity are both unplanned and, at the same time, enduring, they must, first of all, be accepted. No man can deny his family, his race, his national origins. His self-identity, his distinctness from others, and his gift to the total community, lie in his deepening realization of these levels of community. But such acceptance, though obvious, is not easily accomplished. I am rooted in the reality of all my past, in the tradition that comes down to me through my life communities and must now be creatively re-expressed by me and passed on to others. All of this is being human, a person with a past and a future, meeting in a present.

So fundamental is an individual's membership in a life community that failure here can never be compensated on the level of the society or the person community. Comparably, successful incorporation into the family community promises probable success in forming other communities. It is also true that failure of the family community, the racial community, the national community can account for a good part of contemporary man's alienation from himself. It may also account for the over-concern of some people to join societies and form person communities as a compensation for their lack of this basic membership in a life community.

One practical conclusion from this description of the need for membership in the life community is that a person continues to need to be identified with his family, his race, his nation. Neither society, nor the person community can be substitutes for this. To cut a man off from his past is to uproot him and to leave him less able to contribute to society, to participate in person community. The man who is homeless and displaced is less a man and so less capable of community on any level.

Society with its planned activities and regulated goals is a fundamental human possibility. Animals may live in herds; they belong to certain "families" or "tribes"; but they are incapable of a planned union that organizes itself. Man, on the other hand, expresses himself, his communal self, in society. So instinctive is this need that the human person will even form societies that seem to have as their main purpose, simply this expression of man's desire to join in organization with other men. Witness the clubs that children of a certain age level form, just to be part of some organization, or the ritual organization that surrounds some adult clubs.

But societies not only express and incarnate something of man's fundamental need for freely chosen community; they also serve to channel and make more effective an individual's activity. There is so little a man can do by himself that action provides some of the strongest motivation for forming societies. Consequently, the rules of society are action-oriented and because of this they tend to be a-personal, stressing values other than the personal values such as freedom, love, truth. This is not to suggest that societies are necessarily impersonal. They are simply organized along different lines and incorporate other values. Persons, to be fully human, need such organization; to be anti-organization is to attempt to be more than human. In fact, to rule oneself in society is a liberating experience that contributes to the growth of persons, and makes possible that progress of human community that can only come from organized action. Hence the present revolt against structure and organization can be destructive of the very values which protesters profess. Much of the revolt, so widespread today in families, in schools, in churches and even in religious communities, seems to be a kind of compensation for the dictatorial over-regulation of the immediate past. Lack of organization, as many are beginning to discover, can be just as much a tyranny. Society is human and so are rules. But this is true only when a man freely accepts rules and assumes responsibility for them. In this way, society incarnates human community.

Person community and responsibility

A person community has already been described as one in which the members feel responsibility for the group as a whole and co-responsibility for all the others in the group.[3] In other words in a person community the members have bound themselves to each other in love and mutual responsibility so that the salvation of each is the concern of all, and the salvation of all is the concern of each. It is important to understand the meaning and relationship of the terms *love* and *mutual responsibility*. Love is often identified simply with warm sentiment, strong attraction, or basic compatibility of persons. While this is very true, it can have unfortunate results when applied to the love that is the bond of person community. To make such love the identifying bond of community can only lead to disillusion. Only an idealized community can be characterized as a union of persons who are basically compatible, strongly attracted to each other, and capable of warm feelings for all the other members. The reality of person communities is vastly different. Love need not necessarily be described in such terms. Care, concern, mutual responsibility are more realistic expressions for the sort of love that is the bond of person communities. Hence it is more correct to say that mutual responsibility is the concrete expression of love in community and indeed defines that love.

Responsibility, too, is subject to misunderstanding. It can be given a kind of grim note of a sober and steady devotion to duty, a concern for faithful performance of work. Interpreted in this way, responsibility seems almost anti-community or, at best, only one aspect of what persons *owe* to each other. This is evidently too narrow a definition of responsibility and not one on which a notion of person community should be built. Fortunately it is not the only meaning of responsibility.

To be responsible is to be able to respond. And to respond is, first of all, to answer for oneself and, second, to be responsive to what really is. A responsible man is one who can answer for himself and to himself. Every man is a word, having his own meaning. This meaning cannot come from anyone else; it must come from within. But a man can only discover his meaning in relation to others. "The capacity of the self to relate itself to others cannot be achieved by a robust moral will. It is a gift of the original security of the self; that is, it is a matter of 'grace.' "[4]

A responsible man can answer for himself. This means that he can take a stand and can also modify his stand without feeling threatened. He can take care of himself, not with the unrealistic boasting of the frightened child who claims he doesn't need anyone, but with the self-reliance of an adult. The responsible man admits his dependence on others; yet he is not overly dependent to the extent that his whole life is made or threatened in terms of the supportive function of others.

A responsible man can also answer to himself; the approval or disapproval of others is not his final answer. He can disagree without being disagreeable, and his agreement is a considered position, not an easy compromise. When a responsible man makes a promise, his giving of his word is a giving of himself. His response includes recognition of his excuses, when they are really rationalizations; at the same time he is also free enough to make and to accept excuses for real weakness, his own or others.

In short, the responsible man has true potentiality for answering to the real. He can respond to what is and not just react to what appears to be. The difference between responding and reacting can be clarified with a simple example. Suppose that I am threading my way through the crowded aisles of a department store, when I feel a sharp jab in the area of my ribs. My packages start to slip from my grasp; my balance and my dignity are both endangered. My instinctive reaction is to turn around and defend myself from this attack. In fact, I probably do turn around only to be met, in this instance, by the apologetic smile of a harmless little old lady who is even more overburdened than I am. With some effort my reaction turns to response. It was only an accident; no one intended me any harm. So I smile as best I can and answer, "Perfectly all right." I have responded to the reality of the situation.

Reaction, then, is immediate reflex action, based on the way things appear to me. Response is a free answer to what I perceive is the reality buried under these first appearances. Prejudice, for example, is reaction; kindness in the face of difficulties is responsible action.

Community is a union of responsible or responsive persons. The man who enters community must have enough responsibility to answer for himself. He cannot come to community just to be supported by it; he must be a contributing member. He must also have enough confidence in himself to value his contribution for what it is, his own unique response, and this without wasting his time in odious comparisons.

Carl Rogers, in one of his books, describes freedom as "the burden of being responsible for the self one chooses to be." Today, man is being given increased freedom; he must also accept increased responsibility. This is true in general, but perhaps especially true for religious communities. The religious who lives without the immediate authority figure of the local superior, or who discovers that his superior meets his request for permission with a "Use your own judgment," is being given new freedom; he is being asked to be responsible for himself. Similarly, the religious who selects from several job offers and then signs a contract practices a very demanding obedience in response to the Spirit.

In small matters, as well as in greater concerns, the responsibility of religious obedience must include a response to the community. The balance between individual need and community need, between responsibility to and for myself, joined to responsibility to and for community, is a delicate tension that can never be resolved by rule.

The responsible man is free enough to answer to the reality of the others with whom he lives. He is sensitive to needs, even unspoken ones; he responds to others in truth and in love, for truth without love, is irresponsible. Telling another what you think, even when there may be a strong core of truth, can destroy another. The communication of truth is much more than a matter of presenting facts or conveying information; it includes responsibility for helping another to accept and to understand the truth.

In a similar way, love in community can be responsible or irresponsible. Irresponsible love takes on something of the characteristics of reaction. It is immediate and instinctive, based on appearances, and lacks tolerance of the reality that other persons are both lovable and, at times, somewhat difficult to love. It has no patience with the slow growth that makes lasting relationships possible. Irresponsible love often betrays itself in jealousy that turns love back on self and away from real response to the other. Finally, irresponsible love has, as its goal, love itself. It enters into community for the sake of forming I-thou relationships and not for the sake of sharing spiritual values with others.[5] Such motivation is unreal because it expects true love to come from a self-seeking relationship. In contrast, Teilhard de Chardin puts responsible love into a community context. He suggests that "We shall see all, only when we see as one; we shall see one, only when we see from within one another." He goes on to explain that seeing from within another is a responding "heart to heart."[6]

Concretely, responsible love in community expresses itself in response to interpersonal needs. These needs are: inclusion, a sense of belonging; control, both controlling and being controlled; affection, loving and being loved, all of which are just as basic as the primary needs of food, shelter, sleep. They are also needs that a man can receive only as gifts from another. Hence, in community, a man should find a place where he can be at home, relaxed, himself, valued as a person, known and loved. This is to describe man in relation to his primary community, either of family, of the person community, or of his friends. A man also belongs in those wider circles of community where he is not always known personally, but where he is able to respond and to assume responsibility. For a sense of belonging is not only something one receives, it is also something one gives. Each member of the community needs to assume some responsibility for the others who belong. His acceptance of them, his appreciation of their contribution is his positive response to the needs of others to belong to community.

A second area of interpersonal need and consequently of mutual responsibility is the area of control. Interestingly enough, the members of a community need to have some control over what happens in community; they also need to experience some control from the community. To control is to be responsible. To be controlled is also to respond to the reality of living in community. A community without controls is in the process of disintegration, a danger that threatens congregations moving from tight controls to a much more permissive atmosphere. Total permissiveness is, again, irresponsible love. It is a failure of the members to be responsible for the community itself.

Responsible controls, however, must take into consideration the real needs of the individuals and attempt to meet these, along with the needs of the community. Only honest and loving confrontation will make a responsible beginning. Mutual response will make it possible for a man to control himself and, at the same time, to respond to the control expressed by the real needs of the other members of the community and of the community as a whole.

Finally, a community allows its members to respond to each other with affection, to love and be loved. Every man needs to show affection, to have another respond to his affection, to receive affection. Such affection is responsible when it is an honest expression of real love and is free enough to be a man's own answer to the reality of the other. How to show affection in a way that is responsive to one's own temperament, background, capacity for love is something that can only be learned in practice, and community, whether the family community, or the person community is a man's best opportunity for learning. Here he can show affection without embarrassment and receive it in complete openness and trust.

If person community, then, is marked by responsibility, mutual and free, loving and honest, then one criterion for community is clear. Is this community of persons responsible? Are the members growing in ability to answer for themselves as true persons and assuming increasing responsibility for the other members of the community as a whole? Do they respond in truth? Is their love real? Do they answer to and for the inter-personal needs of the community: the need for a sense of belonging, for control and for affection?

When the above can be answered with a strong affirmative, then person community is being formed, and the individuals who make up such a community grow and develop as they respond to the reality of living together responsively.

3 / Forming christian communities

*Christianity means community through Jesus Christ
and in Jesus Christ. No Christian community is
more or less than this. Whether it be a brief, single
encounter or the daily fellowship of years, Christian
community is only this. We belong to one another
only through and in Jesus Christ.*

DIETRICH BONHOEFFER, *Life Together**

ARE OUR COMMUNITIES Christian? Do they originate "in the name of
the Father"? Is what binds us together Christ Jesus, our love of
Jesus, our brother, and of each other? The questions are stark, the
issues so overwhelming that the immediate temptation is to retreat
into meaningless clichés. But these questions are imperative, if we
are to form a Christian community. We can begin our exploration by
relating Christian community to the levels of man's social unity discussed in the previous chapter. On that basis, it would seem that a
community of Christians must have something of the instinctive and
spontaneous emotional unity of the mass; it must also be a life community, a society and, above all, a union of persons.

To say that Christian community is emotional and spontaneous,
meeting man's need for the release of the mass, may seem, at first,
something of an exaggeration. Yet Christian community, like everything human, seeks some form of physical expression. This need is
not just an unpleasant consequence of man's animality, it is also the
sanctifying possibility of the incarnation. Men express emotional

*(New York: Harper & Brothers, 1954), p. 21.

unity by making their presence to each other felt in the warmth of physical closeness. Conversely, they keep their distance when unity is strained. In a similar way, Christians need to feel the support of each other's physical proximity. In fact this is one of the motivating forces in the formation of Christian communities. In a Christian community men feel at home in the presence of fellow Christians. They feel that this is their Father's world; they give thanks together. They express their joy and double it by their sharing. Even when they do not know their fellow Christians personally, still there is the release of mutual participation in common Christian concerns.

Bonhoeffer, who was to know the loneliness of being cut off from his brothers during his imprisonment, writes movingly of this felt need for Christian community.

> The believer feels no shame, as though he were still living too much in the flesh, when he yearns for the physical presence of other Christians. Man was created a body, the Son of God appeared on earth in the body, he was raised in the body, in the sacrament the believer receives the Lord Christ in the body and the resurrection of the dead will bring about the perfected fellowship of God's spiritual-physical creatures. The believer lauds the Creator, the Redeemer, God the Father, Son and Holy Spirit, for the bodily presence of a brother. The prisoner, sick person, the Christian in exile sees in the companionship of a fellow Christian a physical sign of the gracious presence of the triune God. Visitor and visited in loneliness recognize in each other the Christ who is present in the body; they receive and meet each other as one meets the Lord, in reverence, humility and joy. They receive each other's benediction, as the benediction of the Lord Jesus Christ. But if there is so much blessing and joy even in a single encounter of brother with brother, how inexhaustible are the riches that open up for those who by God's will are privileged to live in the daily fellowship of life with other Christians.[1]

In short, Christians need to be together; they need to rejoice in the strength of each other's presence, to know that when they pray, they pray together, and that when they suffer, their pain is part of something bigger than the shrinking world of their own misery. All of this becomes real, however, only through the concrete words and actions of fellow Christians. Christian community embodies this care and concern—"See how they love one another."

A Christian community is also a life community and like every life community its members are united by a bond that is vital and unbreakable. Once a man freely enters into the community of believers, he becomes a Christian in such a real way that he can never repudiate his membership, even were he to cut himself off from visible association. Commitment to the community of faith is a commitment to a life shared with others. Such is the Christian faith by which man believes so strongly in the power of God and the goodness of his brothers, that he is willing to share life with them. Hence, when one member of the Christian community is sick, all suffer; when one member knows new life, all grow and develop. The Christian continues to profess his belief that his brothers are a communion of saints on their way to ever more perfect unity, even when appearances seem to contradict this.

Receiving communion together can be a beautifully expressive sign of a man's willingness to share the same life and be nourished by the same bread, in the same life-community. In the Eucharist, the Christian receives Jesus and all his brothers. So true is this that a man who is not willing to receive his brothers is cautioned to "leave his gift" and go to "be reconciled" before he attempts to receive the Lord Jesus.

As in other life communities, a Christian is joined vitally and irrevocably to his brother, but in contrast to other life communities, a man is not born a Christian, he must choose to become one. This is comparable to his forming a society, and in joining he accepts, at least in a conditional way, an organization and its rules. So too, the Christian finds that membership in the church patterns and regulates his life.

This acceptance of the church as human in its organizational structures seems an essential element of realism for today's Christian. On the one hand, the patterns of church organization are perfectible and therefore changing. Its rules are fallible and so need revision.

Such is the human condition of Christian community expressing itself within the limits of human society. These human limitations are the church's acceptance of failure, as well as its message of hope to other human societies.

> The search for God, as a Christian sees it, is also a search for the right community. The right community does not mean the right church, as much as it means the right kind of church. It is not enough for the church to profess the right faith; it must create a community for the right type of love.[2]

A Christian community is one that seeks to incorporate in its organizational patterns such Christian values as the pre-eminence of the person over the rule, the hierarchy of service rather than of power, the need for solitude along with responsibility for companionship. Like the gospel itself, the Christian community will speak of the delicate balance between "Give back to Caesar what belongs to Caesar—and to God what belongs to God." (Luke 20:25). It will know something of the wisdom of the serpent and the simplicity of the dove. It will be both worldly and other-worldly. Like the gospel, the Christian community, organizing itself as a society, will be for the announcement of "good news." Its rules will be structured around this as its main purpose. Such is the task orientation of the Christian community which will be discussed in a later chapter.

Christian community, then, is for fellowship, for giving life, for sharing the good news. All these express levels of man's social unity: the mass, the life community, the society. But the deepest and truest meaning of Christian community is found in the person community, bonded by mutual responsibility and solidarity of salvation.

Community in Jesus Christ

First of all, Christian person community originates in response to God's call which creates man in such a way that he needs, desires and is able to form community. It is also a response to a Father who seeks the companionship of man, walking in the garden with Adam, calling Abraham to father him a people, and finally sending his Son into the world to make all men one with him and with each other. True response to the Father's call can only come through community in Christ Jesus.

Specifically, a Christian community is one that is formed in Christ; "We belong to one another only through and in Jesus Christ." What does this mean? Bonhoeffer goes on to explain: "It means, first, that a Christian needs others because of Jesus Christ. It means, second, that a Christian comes to others only through Jesus Christ. It means, third, that in Jesus Christ we have been chosen from eternity, accepted in time and united for eternity."[3]

A Christian needs others because of Jesus Christ. If acceptance of one's own poverty is the original conversion of the Christian, then to be a Christian is to be needy and to recognize that this is a state of blessedness. Only the poor man can grow rich in the gift of another; so only a poor man can be enriched by God, saved in Christ Jesus. But this enrichment, this salvation, comes to the Christian through other men. Another accepts a man into the Christian community; another brings him the sacraments; others are the sacrament of Christian community.

Just as Robinson Crusoe on his island would be less than human without his fellow man, so the Christian would be disabled without others. He would have no one to love. The Christian needs his neighbor to express his love of Jesus; he needs his neighbor in order to hear Jesus; and his neighbor needs him in order to communicate the Word of God. Perhaps this is why the truly Christian community will always have a special love for the poor, because the needy give him special opportunities to give, in and through Jesus Christ. And in the same sense every man's poverty is a gift to the Christian community, since it gives others opportunities for generous service.

Second, "a Christian comes to others only through Jesus Christ." As Bonhoeffer goes on to explain, "Without Christ we would also not know our brother, nor could we come to him. The way is

blocked by our own ego. Christ opened up the way to God and to
our brother. Now Christians can live with one another in peace;
they can love and serve one another; they can become one."[4] To
love another man as ourselves is only possible when we have begun
to be redeemed from our selfishness. To love another as brother is
only possible if that other is truly our brother. And he is our brother
in Christ Jesus.

The love of a Christian must be like the love of Christ for us,
"Love one another just as I have loved you" (John 13:34). It must
be a love that reaches out to each and every man. It must be a love
that heals, that seeks by way of preference the sinner, the weak,
the despised, the poor. The love of the Christian must be enduring,
"having loved his own who were in the world, he loved them to
the end" (John 13:1). Ultimately, Christian love must be willing to
give everything, "a man can have no greater love than to lay down
his life for his friends" (John 15:14).

These are the expressions of Christian love in the life of Jesus
Christ himself. Only in Jesus Christ can the Christian live this way.
Against the realism of Christian community, man discovers the
poverty of his love, the meagerness of his response. He measures his
exclusiveness against the all-embracing love of the gospel. He sees
his cowardice and indifference as he passes by his neighbor in need,
his lack of forgiveness when he refuses to rejoice in the return of
the prodigal. He knows how easy it is to turn away from the leper
and seek the clean. The Christian sees again that his love is incon-
stant in the face of constant need. He knows again that a love, costly
of self, is often beyond him.

Living in Christian community, consequently, calls for the
strength of Christ. Only he can make it possible. This is apparent
even on the level of family and close friends. It is perhaps even
more immediately apparent in terms of the total church community,
the world community. In the face of schisms and splits, wars and
national self-seeking, "He is the peace between us" (Eph 2:14). To
live together in love is a gift of God. Our incorporation into Christ
Jesus at baptism gifts us with the Christian possibility of faith and

hope and love. We are able to believe and to trust and to love both God and our brothers.

Finally, a Christian is one who has been "chosen from eternity, accepted in time, and united for eternity" in Christ Jesus. We do not choose our own brothers; such is the truth of human family community; such is the truth of Christian brotherhood.

> Our community with one another consists solely in what Christ has done to both of us. . . . The more genuine and deeper our community becomes, the more will everything else between us recede, the more clearly and purely will Jesus Christ and his work become the only thing that is vital between us. We have one another only through Christ, but through Christ we do have one another, wholly, and for all eternity.[5]

Challenge and consolation. Is Jesus Christ the vital bond between us? Counterfeits ring hollow against the test of such love. What do I ask of my brother? A chance to serve; an opportunity to forgive and be forgiven; a burden to bear with him? If the answer is "Yes," then we are community in Christ and we can look forward to the promise that someday we will be totally for others.

Contrast this realism of Christian community with pious dreams and designs of our own making. We desire a community in which we feel no tension, no pull, and no need to beg God for the grace to do what is beyond our power. We design a community where every other man is perfect and immediately lovable and where we will never learn the meaning of Christian love. We demand of others in the community what God has never demanded of us, and so we become the judges of our brothers and, ultimately, we judge ourselves.

Contemporary man, sharpened in the school of constant criticism, runs the risk of rejecting God's gift because he fails to accept the community that is being offered him: in the church, in his family, in his religious congregation.

> When a person becomes alienated from a Christian community in which he has been placed and begins to raise complaints about it,

he had better examine himself first to see whether the trouble is not due to his wish dream that should be shattered by God; and if this be the case, let him thank God for leading him into this predicament. But if not, let him nevertheless, guard against ever becoming an accuser of the congregation before God. Let him rather accuse himself for his unbelief. Let him pray God for an understanding of his own failure and his particular sin, and pray that he may not wrong his brethren. Let him, in the consciousness of his own guilt, make intercession for his brothers. Let him do what he is committed to, and thank God.[6]

In the face of the rising divorce rate, greater numbers of canonical leaves of absence, and public statements from those desiring to separate themselves from the church, Bonhoeffer's balanced view has new urgency. On the one hand, he admits that, at times, it will be the individual who will have failed; but at other times it will be the community's responsibility. In either case, the individual cannot afford to place himself outside the sinning community, nor can the community deny its responsibility for, in some senses, failing the individual. In community all stand in solidarity of salvation. All need God's mercy and the forgiveness of the brethren.

Signs of Christian community

Since Christian community is community in and through Jesus Christ, it will be marked by the signs of Christ's own life: incarnation, passion and resurrection.

To say that Christian community is incarnate is to suggest that it is both divine and human, both spirit and body. Like everything bodied, the human community will be structured in certain definite ways, and these structures will both express the spirit of the community and, at the same time, shape this spirit. Human community will have to be realized within limitations of space, of time, and of size. It will be culturally conditioned and, therefore changing. On the one hand, it will be responsible for adapting only what is best in contemporary culture; on the other hand, it will have to adapt itself, more or less, to the culture in which it finds itself. Since human community will be bodied in the lives of individual persons, it will be essentially pluralistic: one community differing from another; each community including a variety of needs, desires, even of ideas as to what community is all about. Incarnate community, like everything bodied, will always be a reaching out to others. Communities are formed in response to certain needs; they remain strong and vigorous as long as this goal orientation is evident. They begin to falter when their purpose for being is no longer clear and compelling. Then community risks turning back in on itself, a kind of narcissism that will reduce a community to childish self-interest.

A second sign of Christian community is the mark of the cross. Suffering need not divide a community; it can be a tremendous force for unified strength. In the face of crisis a community discovers itself anew. It can come to greater understanding of suffering in the world and may ultimately emerge from its period of trial purified and more sensitive to the whole meaning of redemption. But all this takes faith, and faith is its own kind of suffering: the pain of the "not-yet," the deliberate affirmation in the face of doubt; the resistance of the temptation to set up tests and make demands. Community asceticism is another mark of the passion for the Christian. To live closely with others is truly an asceticism, one that flows out of charity and not from some self-designed form of discipline. Communal asceticism comes from the demands of living in community; it also helps to form community. It arises out of the life-style of the community and, at the same time, gives a certain style and shape to this life together. A Christian community will be one that has faced certain temptations, that has been tried and not been found wanting. Just as the temptations of Christ marked the beginning of his ministry, so too a community will find itself tried in relation to its very identity and mission. It will be tempted by the demands of service to forget that it is community; it will sometimes be tested in its dedication to others, by its very desire to be community. But out of these temptations a community will form itself in greater integrity and renewed dedication.

If forming Christian community implies suffering, growth takes place through faith, self-discipline, and ultimately the test of temptations from within and without. Still Christian community only begins here. The end of Christian community is the joy of resurrection and new life. Even here and now, Christian community is one of faith and of hope. In community, man finds hope when he feels personal despair; in community, man's hope for heaven knows at least some transitory promise of realization. To hope together is to pray together. For man by himself is hopeless. Only with God and with others can a man find himself and learn to live in peace. And this is to respond to God in prayer. In prayer a man is able to respond for the whole Christian community, for his immediate personal community, for himself. His prayer is truly prayer when it is response to the Spirit who "pleads for us with unutterable groanings." When Christians join together in prayer, they experience even here and now something of the fruits of true Christian community: "charity, joy, peace, patience." They begin to realize the truth— "How good, how delightful it is for all to live together like brothers" (Ps 133).

4 / Structuring community

.... *a gentle structure*
that supports just enough so that the thing can go up.
A good structure makes freer than no structure
                    because it supports
but very soon when the thing is built the structure is dissolved
or should be replaced by another structure.

SISTER CORITA, *Footnotes and headlines**

TO SPEAK OF human community is to speak of something structured,
something bodied. For human community, like man himself, is both
spirit and body, not two things joined together in an uneasy marriage, but two principles forming one unity. Just as philosophers
have always wrestled more or less successfully with the exact nature
of body-soul relationships, so too the question of spirit and structure
in community remains a debated issue.

That soul and body or spirit and structure form a unity, the human person, and that these two divergent principles interact, are
matters of everyday experience. Spirit shapes body, and body shapes
and expresses spirit. To neglect one is to neglect the other. To over-
emphasize one is to diminish the other and ultimately to risk the
destruction of both.

These rather obvious truths about the human person are equally
applicable to human community. The spirit of a community is expressed in its structures; these structures, in turn, shape as well as
express the spirit of the community. To over-emphasize structure is

*(New York: Herder and Herder, 1967), p. 8.

to deaden spirit. To attempt to form community without structure is to pretend to be more than human.

In the immediate past, the greater danger was an over-emphasis on structure: rules, constitutions, customs, regulating almost all the details of human life, with great value placed on conformity, uniformity and ritual. Today, the danger lies in a desire so to minimize structure that the body loses support and strength. This contemporary trend seems in part a compensation for the excessive structures of the past. Surely, many of the structures of the past needed revision. But it is always easier to tear down than to build. So in the post-Vatican II period there are many structures that must be eliminated; but the painful labor of building new structures is equally imperative.

Principles of structure building

Building always calls for blueprints, laying out the essential designs of the new structure and specifying the materials to be used in construction. This chapter will attempt to suggest some principles which should shape new structures for renewed communities. It will also indicate a few of the components of the new construction.

An explanation and something of an apology is necessary before beginning with principles. Only general principles can be given, and this as a matter of principle. Communities themselves must determine appropriate structures. A detailed rule of life, if it is to be a living thing, must come from the individual. It must express him, his needs and, at the same time, it must provide sufficient discipline and direction to make effective the contribution of this individual in all his uniqueness of spirit.

The two principles which pre-eminently determine renewed community structures are those of subsidiarity and collegiality. According to subsidiarity decisions must be made at the lowest possible level so that what affects the individual must be decided by the individual; what affects the local community must be determined by that local community and so on to the highest levels of government. In short, appropriate structures must be determined by those who will have to live with them. And they must be determined in a collegial manner so that the community, together, arrives at a decision through the dialectic of agreement-disagreement, resulting in eventual consensus. Although this will result in some delays, confusion, and messy situations, these negative aspects, presently being experienced, can be minimized, if subsidiarity and collegiality are structured into the workings of the community and not left up to the goodwill and initiative of the moment. We shall come back to this point in a subsequent section of this chapter.

Even after proper structures have provided opportunities for subsidiarity and collegiality to function effectively, the resulting lack of uniformity will threaten many people. In fact, the distinction between the uniformist and the pluriformist attitude to community structures may be a more adequate expression of what divides communities today, than the more familiar labels of conservative and liberal. The uniformists feel threatened by the differences inherent in any application of subsidiarity and collegiality. Assurances that "Just because other individuals, other local communities determine a certain life-structure, this does not require you to change," fail to reassure the uniformists. It is not just their practices that are threatened, but their fundamental value system, which identifies community with equality and sameness of structure. Although it is quite easy to sympathize with the uniformist, his position seems to be based on notions of community that are no longer valid. If community is identified with full growth of human persons, then it must find expressions in structures which are person-oriented and so pluralistic.

To say that community structures must be person-oriented is to suggest what has been said so many times: renewal of structures will only be effective in terms of a renewal of persons. But renewal of persons is either helped or hindered by structure. This point is missed if a community hopes to begin with spiritual renewal and only then move into changing structures, and also if a community spends all its time and effort on renewal of structures and hopes that renewal of dedication will follow. Persons cannot be renewed without renewal of structure, and revitalizing structure presupposes the vitality of the individuals who live in these structures. So a double offensive is the only realistic possibility.

Another consequence of the person orientation of renewed community structures is the realization that these structures must be both human and humanizing. A human structure, for one thing, is always a changing structure. More accurately, human structures evolve. They come out of a past and must be related to that past. They point to a future, and in pointing to what lies ahead they underline their own transitoriness. In short, human structures change gradually but continuously. Hence the hopes of those who are waiting for a time when "things will settle down again" are vain. Such attempts to "stop the world" are based, perhaps, on the long delayed change of past structures; they fail to take into account that overdue change is an argument in favor of constant change.

Human structures are, then, open structures. They are open to their own re-structuring. They open a man to the world, to his fellow man, to God. Any structure that fails this test of openness must be revised. This is not to suggest that structures must be so open-ended that they no longer structure. *To open* suggests that something may also be *closed,* but closed only for the sake of a more complete opening like a store "closed on Wednesday" but "open all day Saturday." So community structures safeguard privacy for the sake of greater community and provide for some quiet and withdrawal in order to permit deeper involvement.

This rhythm of withdrawal and engagement, of reflection and expression, is an essential humanizing aspect of community structures. The proportion of reflection and expression is determined by the spirit of the individual and the needs of the local community, and is also related to the needs of the wider community. Hence structure must be flexible, open to these changing needs and differing spirits.

Human structures, if they are to be fully humanizing, must be meaningful. In a sense, a meaningless structure is no structure at all;

it is only an object. Structures embodying spirit must have a meaning for the persons whose life and activity are being formed by them. If a structure is not meaningful, it should be rejected. Structure for structure's sake is meaningless; like everything that is significant, structure takes on meaning only in terms of persons.

In almost every case, structure can be presupposed to have had meaning at the time of its origin. The question remains: what does it mean now? If the answer is "Nothing," then this particular form is already dead and awaiting burial. Before rejecting any structure, however, it might be well to try to discover its original meaning so that this meaning can now be embodied in some more appropriate form. Otherwise something meaningful may be lost, and spirit impoverished.

Discovering the meaning of structures requires dialogue within community, since shared meaning is the presupposition of community structures.[1] Such dialogues about the re-structuring of community life require broad based participation, freedom of communication, and realized responsibility. Past failures, present successes, and future needs must be common concerns, if they are to give rise to meaningful structures. Such openness and sharing of needs is the opposite of a reserve and secrecy destructive of community.

To re-structure a community requires leadership. Sometimes it is thought that collegiality is a denial of leadership. Actually it is more a denial of authoritarianism than of authority. In a collegial community it is one of the roles of the leader (and in a collegial community of personally responsible members all are, to some extent, leaders) to raise questions about the meaning of structures, so that unmeaningful structures can be renewed, and enduring values be given new embodiment.

Once the question about the meaning of structures has been answered, it is the role of authority to initiate the consideration of changes. This is to say that the leader is one who is responsible for getting new structures into operation, allowing sufficient time for a realistic appraisal and, finally, ensuring that such an appraisal is followed up by consequent adjustments of structures. Lacking such leadership, structures will simply deteriorate; nothing will replace them, and the result will be a shapeless community.

Though change requires initiative from someone acting as a leader, it also requires a kind of community consensus. Such a consensus grows out of a process of continuing education and formation. Structures which need constant updating help to make real an education in the principles of the community, for it is only after a principle has been embodied in a structure that it can be realized and evaluated.

Finally, the question of how much structure is needed is an issue that cannot be settled in the abstract, for it is a matter of practical living. What can be suggested are some of the symptoms indicative of too much or too little structure. "Over-structuring results in legalism, scrupulosity, compulsiveness. Too little structure brings on a certain loss of identity and consequent uprootedness and anxiety."[2] On the basis of these symptoms, a diagnosis can be made along with some prescription leading to a cure.

In principle, then, community structures should be based on subsidiarity and collegiality, with the exact structuring left to determination by the communities affected. Such structures, embodying the spirit of different communities, will be plural in form. They will also be person-oriented, human, and humanizing. As such they will be changing, evolving; they will be open and meaningful. Their meaning will be determined through community dialogue and, when they are no longer meaningful, they will have to be replaced by some newer form which will incorporate valid values from the past.

Suggested structures for renewed communities

The principles of subsidiarity and collegiality are critically important in any attempt to renew community structures. These principles, in fact, must themselves be incorporated into the structures of the community if they are to function effectively and not remain idealistic values. This means that members of local communities must be given opportunities to meet together to determine appropriate structures. If such opportunities for collegial decisions are not provided, the group will either be structureless or certain "strong" individuals will take over and have their way with the group.

To prevent either of these alternatives, both equally destructive of true community, one option would be the structuring of certain times and places where the group could meet to criticize or give new meaning to existing structures, and to determine new ones. Such meetings will allow the members to function responsibly within the community and not to fragment it through useless criticism, which fails to change anything. For example, when a group comes together, say at the beginning of a new school year, or when new members join a local community, or when there is a change in leadership in the community, the members need an opportunity to consider themselves as a community and to determine appropriate forms of expressing community through structure. Such reflection of a community on its own identity takes time. But it seems that local communities have a serious need of sitting down together and drawing up some community-determined policies on matters that concern the total local group.

What is of concern to a local community? This very question could be the first item on the agenda for this suggested set of initial community meetings. One concern that should have high priority would be the determination of how this particular community should provide opportunities for its members to meet. No matter what form of local government is determined, either by higher authority or by the choice of the local group, still the community as a whole needs to take periodic stock of itself. Opportunities for this should be scheduled, otherwise such meetings become emergency measures and, to that extent, are failures in communication even before they begin.

If every member of the local community is to assume responsibility for the community as a whole as well as for himself, then he needs to know what these responses should be. Since in an age of grow-

ing personal freedom and complexity of rapid changes these responsibilities cannot be formalized, they must be determined by the
individual members in dialogue with each other. Again, an initial
set of meetings can help to determine these areas of responsibility.
Once determined they can and should be set down, not so that they
become set and unchangeable, but simply as criteria or standards,
which must, then, be constantly re-evaluated, again by the group
acting together. This process of constant re-evaluation is another
principle which should be structured into a community's on-going
expression of itself. For if new structures become hardened, they are
soon no better than the structures they replaced. And today the
situation might even become worse, since rapid change makes new
forms obsolete in a very short space of time.

An individual needs an opportunity to present very simply and
honestly his understanding, or lack of understanding, of his responsibilities. He needs to accept his failures in responsibility and to
know that these failures are accepted by the community because he
is accepted. The local community, as a group, needs to reaffirm or
to change its initially determined policies, to determine new structures to meet new demands. The larger community: the area, the
region, the province, the congregation as a whole, also needs structures providing for periodic re-evaluation. Such re-evaluation is one
of the primary functions of chapter or senates. These collegial bodies
must meet at regular and rather frequent intervals so that on-going
change becomes part of community structure and not a disruptive
crisis measure.

For both local community and larger community, the success of
such re-evaluation will be determined, in large measure, by the representative quality of the opinions sampled. In the local community
every member must be encouraged to speak; in fact, this need to
contribute to the community's on-going evaluation of itself must be
seen as one of an individual's most pressing responsibilities. In the
larger community, representation of elected or appointed delegates
is a prime consideration, and structuring for such representation is a
difficulty of both large and small communities. Again on the local

level, drawing up an agenda to which each member is invited to contribute his suggestions will ensure a representative sampling of topics to be covered. During the meeting itself, members can be asked to make a statement of view on items of some importance. This will provide opportunities for the less aggressive to speak . . . and for the more aggressive to listen.

On the level of the larger community, representation that will ensure a fair and balanced evaluation is not easily come by. Democratic elections are not the automatic solution, for this procedure may result in a most unrepresentative combination of people: those who have held prominent positions in the community, who are popular, who do work which brings them into contact with many of the electors. Such elections may result in a whole segment of the community lacking representation, and experts, whose skills are badly needed, may be excluded from the chapter. Perhaps some combination of election and appointment of representatives will ensure the fairest form of evaluation.

How often such policy-making groups should meet is another matter of initial determination. It is also necessary to determine what procedure should be used if any member or group of members feels a need for a specially called meeting. Too many meetings, considering too many trivial items, chip away at the patience and attention of the members. Meetings that come too infrequently stagger under the load of business to be accomplished and eventually give up what is clearly impossible.

Another matter to be decided by the community is the whole area of accountability. In what specific matters is the individual accountable to the local community? The local community to higher authority? Higher authority to the chapter? Accountability for such items as management of finances, job-performance, and plans for undertaking new kinds of work are some areas where subsidiarity also involves accountability to higher authority. Such accountability is not primarily a way of checking on individual performance; it is a way of allowing the individual to exercise responsibility by presenting an account for approval by the community. This positive aspect of accountability needs to be made effective if individuals are to overcome their fear of meddling and misunderstanding. Accountability is intended to provide safeguards for the individual as well as for the community. This will become more real, if it is no longer a matter of higher authority calling the individual to account, but rather of the individual knowing, through carefully predetermined srtuctures, precisely what he is accountable for.

Another structure needed for the successful functioning of a collegial community is some kind of board of appeals. Even though the principle of subsidiarity is clear enough (what effects the individual should be determined by the individual and what effects the community should be determined by the community), still the practice, at times, becomes confusing and even dangerous for both individual and community. A strong individual may threaten the rights of the community; the community, in its turn, may be negligent of the needs of the individual. When this kind of conflict occurs, it is too late to work out a system of appeals; this must be built into the structure of the community, if there is to be impartiality. A board of appeals is a structure with which communities have little or no experience but it is needed to balance out the sometimes conflicting objectives of individual and community.

In all of the above there has been a recurrent theme of the need for structures to change. This suggests a needs for experimentation as part of structure. In short, experimentation needs to be built into the structures of renewing communities. Experiments should not follow on need and crisis; they should anticipate problems, providing a range of possible solutions for questions that are just beginning to be asked.

Such experimentation calls for initiative, for creative thinking, and for practical action, accompanied by some degree of risk. These demands are too expensive to be left to chance determination, emergency planning. Local communities, councils, and chapters should encourage experimentation, providing opportunities for the creative individual to present his ideas, obtain a critical evaluation of them, and gain help in carrying them out and ultimately evaluating them.

In the last few years, the call for renewal has created some structures for initiating and evaluating experimentation. But these structures seem to concentrate on minimizing risk and providing "safe" forms of experiments. Now there is need for more creative forms, for the acceptance of experimentation as a permanent contribution of religious congregations to the pilgrim church.

Another more everyday need is for structures that provide opportunities to communicate and to learn and develop communication skills. Training in group dynamics, in techniques for leading and taking active part in discussions—these are experiences which need to be structured into a community's program for on-going formation and not just provided for on a hit and miss basis. Such skills cannot create communication or community, but they can make their realization more possible.

Along with providing for training in techniques, community structures should also provide opportunities for members to communicate with each other as individuals, as small groups, as a total group. The communication of member to member is not a threat to community; it is its very life-blood.

Communication is contingent upon the question of leisure. How much leisure is needed to form community? The very mention of leisure is something of a joke to today's religious, caught up, as so many are, in a constant succession of meetings, committees, and commitments. Yet leisure is an absolute necessity for individual persons and for communities. Without leisure, persons become work-producing machines and communities become hotels where people live as they move from one job to another. Because leisure tends to be a neglected element in community formation, there is additional need to structure for it. In the past, community recreation, at least in intent if not in practice, was an attempt to provide leisure for community. Unfortunately, a structure centered around uniform time and place often did not recreate the community.

Since communities differ so much one from the other, they need to structure ways for a particular local group to celebrate leisure together. Again this structure must be community determined. Forms helpful in providing community recreation might include: budgeting for relaxation, encouraging members to take time to cultivate individual interests, sharing leisure time projects with other members of the community, giving members the freedom and encouragement to spend some of their leisure time with members of their professional communities and with other friends who share similar interests and hobbies.

Sensitivity to another's need for leisure is a whole area of community responsibility where again persons can learn both to give and to receive. Here religious communities can fill their role of experimental, future-oriented groups, looking ahead to the needs of families and civic communities in an age of increasing leisure.

Central to any renewal of religious structures is concern with persons rather than with matters of time and location. In the past the local community has frequently been just that: a group of persons who found themselves living together in the same place, working in the same place. But newer notions of community suggest other ways of structuring it. If a community can be described as a group of persons whose presence to each other makes a difference, then it may be suggested that religious communities be structured in more imaginative ways. As Gabriel Moran suggests, "The religious congregation, one would suppose, would be an excellent place to try to realize communities other than on a local basis."[3] Increasingly variant apostolates, more and more religious engaged in special works will probably hasten experimentation along the lines of the non-local community. Hopefully, the needs of a world where more and more people find themselves constantly on the move but still wanting to be part of a community can also be a motivating force.

The question of size of community is another matter for self-determined structures. One practical criterion suggested is that the community should be small enough so that personal relationships can be felt. It should be of such a size to permit true communication, not just the passing on of information but personal communication of the Christian experience. Information can, of course, be communicated via the bulletin board and the office memo. But what is personal cannot be communicated by such impersonal mechanisms. So there are very real and much discussed limits as to how large a community can be. There are also limitations as to how small it can be. A community is too large, when the members cannot respond to each other's personal needs because they lack opportunity for discovering these needs; it is too small, when these needs, even when they are known, cannot be met because the community lacks resources. The trend today seems to be toward smaller communities, not only smaller local communities but also smaller congregations. The disadvantages of smallness can be compensated through federation and structures providing for inter-community sharing. On the other hand, larger communities can be organized, as Eugene Kennedy suggests, into "subgroups or subcommunities which enable the development of compatible and healthy relationships and which are allowed to function with a good deal of autonomy. A good starting point would be to divide communities according to the interests and preferences of the members."[4] Perhaps the point of common concern around which the community, large or small, should be organized is shared philosophy on what community is all about. Then structures can follow spirit, rather than trying, sometimes vainly, to engender it.

A final suggestion as to renewed structures concerns the purpose of rules in religious life today. In the past rules, constitutions, customs were *the* structural supports of religious life. Today, when detailed directives are left to local decision and are open to constant re-evaluation, the purpose of rule must also be reconsidered. Moran explains that:

> A rule or constitution should exist not as a thing to be enforced but as a guarantee of the rights of the individual and the rights of the group. A person entering into life with a group ought to know the ideals of the group and the procedures of its organization. A society, in its turn, needs a way to specify responsibilities to members and deal with individuals who are not responsive.[5]

So rule attempts to express something of the goals of a group and to provide an expression of these which will consider both individual members and the group as a whole. A community is a group of persons who not only love Christ but love him together. A rule attempts to say how.

This *how* must be kept open and flexible. It must also be in some way structured collegially, constantly undergoing re-evaluation, expressing accountability and allowing for appeals. Such community structuring calls for experimentation, communication, leisure, smaller communities and a shared philosophy of what community is all about. In this way renewed community structures will provide "gentle support" for forming new communities.

5 / Pluralism and community

*Can we find a way to let people be themselves
and do what they choose to do, while, at the
same time, have people live with each other
in peace, justice and love?*
GABRIEL MORAN, *Experiences in Community**

IN OUTLINING what he calls one of the chief problems of our society, Moran puts his finger on a critical issue for renewing communities. Pluralism is a fact of our society; or perhaps better, it is an irreversible process. What are the consequences of pluralism for community? Are the two concepts, in a sense, antithetical, so that increasing pluralism results in diminished community? Is there a crisis point where the toleration of pluralism threatens to destroy community? Finally, granted that some degree of pluralism is a fact of life for today's community, what will be the consequences? What will be the face and shape of a community formed in pluralism?

The reality of pluralism

In a sense pluralism is at the heart of community. A community made up of persons must be rich in the variety of its individual

*(New York: Herder and Herder, 1968), p. 45.

members. Each person brings a unique element of difference and divergence to community. The fact of pluralism, therefore, is nothing new. What is new is a welcoming of pluralism and a concentration on a unity that will allow for differences, in contrast to previous attempts to minimize differences for the sake of uniformity. These polarities run through all of contemporary society. On the one hand, man wants to wipe out differences and inequalities: between the *haves* and *have-nots*, between black and white, within ethnic groups and religious sects. No man wants to live in a ghetto surrounded only by those like himself in background, race, religion, or any other artificial means of division. At least, no man wants to be forced to live in isolation from the creative differences that are part of an open society.

On the other hand, the man of today places a premium on being himself, on being allowed to do "his thing." Every man asserts his uniqueness and guards the secret that is himself. He seeks the privacy of being himself, and yet he desires the community of being with others. He is equally angered by anything that keeps him from expressing himself and by anything that prevents him from being as good as anybody else.

A distinction between artificial and personal differences is one way of reconciling what, at first, appear to be contradictory needs. Persons must differ if they are to be themselves, if they are to enter into community with all the personal riches that each can bring when he is most himself. On the other hand, artificial differences, especially formalisms that are imposed from without and so are unrelated to personal freedom, are to be rejected as destructive of personal community. What is accepted is a pluralism that welcomes those differences which promote true community; what is rejected is a uniformity that destroys the richness of variety in community.

In a period when there was less emphasis on person, pluralism was an almost unknown value. The ideal was to discover the "best" solution, the "truest" answer, the "ideal religious." Once such models were formulated, then it was simply a matter of conforming to the pattern. Such is the essentialist's approach expressed in such concerns as "What is a saint?" "What is the nature of religious life?" "What are the essential differences between a religious congregation and a secular institute?" "Answers" are found in manuals of spirituality, catechisms of the vows, and in carefully detailed books of customs. Against such an "idealist" background, conformity becomes a highly prized religious practice, and uniformity is valued as a criterion of community. This model, so carefully detailed, provides incentive for personal striving, along with satisfaction of some degree of perceptible achievement. Uniformity makes for an orderly world where men have, at least, some common answers to value questions.

Today's changing world view has chipped away at this model theory and left man insecure in his search. "Answers" are now seen as tentative attempts to formulate values; and like all human formulations, these value statements are somewhat inadequate and highly personal. They reflect what is seen by man from his own particular background, the limitations imposed on him by time and by place. If "answers" are now seen as highly personal and only tentative, then conformity is no longer an ideal either; in fact, it is something of a danger because it inhibits the individual in his own search for mature and responsible freedom and risks having the community follow blindly the value judgments of a few limited persons. For this generation the price of conformity comes too high.

Freedom of expression, of personal decision, the right to dissent, all ensure that contemporary communities will be pluralistic. But pluralism has its own inherent dangers. External pluralism can provide a disguise for hidebound conformism. By way of comparison, just as children may seek security in similarity, so too adolescents may fall victim to a patterned response of rebellion. Both are immature. Difference for the sake of difference is no better than uniformity for the sake of sameness. What is at stake is not so much uniformity or diversity but the freedom of a responsible person to decide for himself whether he should dissent or conform. And this in the context of community.

Pluralism and community

To mention community in the same sentence with plurality and uniformity is to expose conflict. Granted that the individual person needs to be himself, to discover and to express his own response to reality, is not the resulting pluralism destructive of community? For example, the almost endless controversy over religious habit and veil; the difficulties experienced by religious who express interest in other works besides those traditionally identified with community apostolate; the desires, the need of so many for detailed guidelines, all seem related to the fundamental threat of pluralism in community.

To return to the basic fact, a certain element of pluralism in community can never be controverted. Different people have different needs: physical, psychological, spiritual. Any attempt to respond to such unequal needs with a measurably equal response must begin and end in injustice. The inequality of giving an equal portion of food to every member of the community is an obvious example and one that has almost always been admitted in practice. What is not so readily admitted is the equally necessary inequality of response to differing psychological and spiritual needs. Each person has unique desires and needs; his needs are also different at different times in his life; the predominance of physical or psychological or spiritual needs is another aspect of fundamental pluralism of persons in community.

To refuse a request because, "If I give this to you, I will have to give it to everyone else," is to reduce community to the level of childish demands. "To each according to his needs; from each according to his capacity" is one of the truths that a pluralistic culture might accept from Karl Marx. Here is a very real test of each man's maturity for community. For it means that inequality is built into community. Some individuals will be more responsive than others; some will have to assume more responsibility, others less. The old will have to be generous in responding to the needs of the young, even in the face of the undeniable fact that their own comparable needs were not met in their youth. And the young will have to shoulder responsibilities that another generation never faced and, perhaps, does not even recognize as responsibilities for today. In short, changing circumstances call for changing response and so for pluralism in forming community.

Granted, such pluralism and built-in inequality will create some problems, as the sharp edges of differences between persons begin to rub against each other. What one man desires another will despise. What one man considers a need another will view as luxury or even waste. The needs of one person will run counter to the desires of another. What is only desire for one man will be deep-seated need in another. This will be hard to understand, especially for the individual who finds his desire sacrificed to another's need.

In the past, such areas of potential conflict were community-oriented in the sense that they were community determined choices. Rules and regulations, directives, and customs programmed suitable responses and so cut down on difference and conflict. Today the free choices of the religious man living in a pluralistic community must also be community oriented choices. This is to suggest that true pluralism is the direct opposite of individualism. "To be oneself" and "to do what one chooses to do" without regard for other men is to destroy oneself and to lose freedom. Selfishness is always self-defeating. Just as an individual man must seek to balance his physical, psychological, and spiritual needs and make his peace with strong drives for privacy countered by equally powerful needs for society, so too he must learn how to live in a community of widely different and sometimes conflicting interests. This calls for new skills to form renewed communities.

For one thing it calls for freedom in expressing oneself. Only known needs can be met. A need that is hidden and then becomes cause for complaint against the community has an element of self-deception about it. Individuals in communities have always been encouraged to make their needs known; but often the encouragement given before the need is presented is withdrawn when the request proves to be too troublesome.

To speak of one's needs, even of one's desires, is an expression of realistic humility. It is to reveal oneself, to expose oneself. It is also an opportunity for self-knowledge. A need that is kept to oneself has a tendency to soak up self-pity and so expand. A need exposed is kept in proportion; it may even shrink in the saying.

To receive the needs of others and to listen to their desires is a kind of self-emptying that is part of self-giving. Not that every expressed need and desire must be accepted and met. Every man needs others to help him sort out need from desire, unreal needs from real needs. We all have blind spots that prevent us from seeing; we all find ourselves more or less deaf to what runs counter to our own interests. Worst of all, part of this blindness and deafness is longstanding habit or unconscious selfishness that cannot be met on the level of simple, self-originating resolution. It must be met by the honesty of friends in community.

Simply to expose another's selfishness or one's own—is not the same as to cure it, just as surgery may or may not bring health. Selfish desires need more than the honesty of another to reveal them for what they are; they also need the love of another, if such surgery is to result in healing. Not that this honesty, this loving acceptance must always come in terms of spoken appraisal of another. Very often, the context of community alone is sufficient to cure a man's blindness, to improve his hearing. What may seem a matter of urgent need to the individual himself becomes of secondary importance once he begins to perceive the more pressing needs of others. Desires have a tendency to fade in the face of another's bread and butter requirements.

Only when members of a community are willing to reveal something of their personal needs and desires on the physical, the psychological, the spiritual level, can this kind of shared response become a reality. But such revelation, costly as it will always be, requires an atmosphere of sensitivity and acceptance. Sometimes, it is only by trying to put his own needs into words that an individual begins to understand them. It is only in being given the freedom to satisfy some of his desires than an individual can discover for himself that these are ersatz attempts at self-satisfaction. Sometimes a flimsy excuse may cover for a real need to discover something about oneself. On the other hand, a desire for spiritual things may be a form of compensation for personal insecurity. It is only in sharing that all this plurality of needs and desires of differing individuals can be put into the context of community. There they can make for unity, rather than division; strength and honesty, against selfishness and weakening forms of compensation.

One of the very real concerns expressed by those who fear pluralism is the risk of losing identity as a community. They ask: "Who will we be, if every member of the community expresses himself in a different apostolate, different dress, different life-style?" In the face of such pluralism, some religious have already concluded in a kind of despair; "We *are* no longer a community." Such fears, of course, are rooted in past conceptions of community, identifying it with common life, where everybody did pretty much the same thing, at the same time and in the same way. But such fears are also very much part of present and future differences in the meaning of community. As has already been pointed out in a previous chapter, the meaning of community is analogous. Even the modified phrase "person community" is still open to as many different interpretations as there are different people living in such communities.

One of the dangers that Moran perceptively warns against is that of identifying community with the description given by today's liberals.[1] Though the contemporary viability of communities which are tightly structured, "removed from the world" and uniform in observance, may be questioned, such communities have a right to discover their own future. If pluralism is a principle of community, then it must be applied to all the variant forms of community. If there are persons who see community as just described, then they should be free to live it, as they conceive it, but not to impose it on others.

This brings up the delicate question of just how many concepts of community can be accepted, how many life-styles approved within one community. Can one and the same congregation find room for totally different life-styles? Can a single local group contain persons who have totally different concepts of the basic meaning of religious life and still call itself a community? These are some of the most vexing questions concerning religious today.

The first problem of totally different life-styles in the same congregation seems somewhat easier, since there is some present experience that can be brought to bear upon it. Religious communities are already familiar, at least to some extent, with the workings of federation. Within the last five years such federations, encouraged by Vatican II, have increased in number. Hopefully, they are on their way to becoming increasingly effective on the grassroots level in the lives of individual religious. In such federations, congregations of quite different spirit and structure are learning to work together for their common good. They are discovering, in a very reassuring manner, that they have common problems and that they can work together toward more effective solutions. If this kind of sharing is possible between different congregations, it seems logical to conclude that it could be affected between different local communities, federated into the same religious congregation.

Such may well be the direction of the future, as local communities, through the implementation of subsidiarity, are given increasing right to decide things for themselves. Such communities will have widely different life-styles; perhaps quite different philosophies of community. What they will share will be such things as richness of personnel resources, services that go beyond the capacity of any one local group, as well as certain minimal structures which make such sharing possible. For instance, certain structures of government will give direction to the efforts of the total community and provide an overview of needs, preventing the local community from becoming too "provincial."

This still leaves unanswered the question of just how much pluralism can be incorporated into the local community itself before it ceases to be *a* community. Certainly this is not an unusual problem.

The experience of having many sub-groups, living in the same larger community is not a new one. What may be new is the sharpness of these divisions, their inevitability, as well as their public recognition. In the past such sub-groupings were often discouraged, classified as cliques, and consequently driven underground. Today, these differences are not only matters of personality groupings; they are often based on fundamental differences as to how religious life should be lived.

There are times when such differences become so sharp that the members of the community spend a disproportionate amount of psychic energy trying to live in something like exterior peace. As a consequence their apostolate is impoverished, and personalities crumble under the strain. Intra-community relationships can degenerate into a constant haggling over a thousand trivia, resulting in apathy, bitterness, sometimes hatred; at which point there is no longer pluralism, because there is no longer any real openness. And there is no real community.

The question remains: is such degeneration into a kind of psychic violence the only possible outcome of radical difference of belief within a community? Or can the living together of open-minded persons lead to still richer concepts of community, embodying both the old and the new? Here is an area where further experimentation is particularly needed. Can strong local communities be built by people whose "communality" is a shared desire to build community? Or, to be successful, must a group of community builders begin with some basic agreement as to what community is all about? In one experiment, the local house could be made up of people who are willing to experiment but who do not necessarily agree on the shape of a successful community. Another group could be selected on the basis of compatible philosophies of community.

Sometimes objections are raised, in principle, to forming communities of compatible people. "After all, anyone could live in community with people who were in basic agreement with oneself," runs one such objection. But what is being proposed is not a community of self-sorted friends, only a grouping of people whose philosophy of community is compatible. It may also be suggested that even if a community were to be formed of persons who were already friends, or who were to become friends in the course of the experiment, this is not a matter for suspicion. To live in community with friends, is, on the one hand, an ideal to be worked for; on the other hand, it is an opportunity to grow through shared suffering. It is never particularly easy; just particularly worthwhile.

A more serious set of objections to forming community through careful groupings is the fact that it may be premature. "In any social reform, premature unity is worse than conflict."[2] This is true because it eliminates the creativity that can bring something new out of two opposing points of view. It also risks letting people harden in their present positions, rather than providing them with daily occasions for broadening their present point of view.

The question of groupings, based on what is most personal to man, his beliefs, and the way he expresses these beliefs in variant life-styles, is an issue that is much broader than the religious congregation. It is one that threatens to split the church itself. Witness the strong statement of Rosemary Reuther, "We see that Roman Catholicism as a 'communion' is a legal fiction. Our schism, then, is not merely one of culture but of faith. It is an estrangement of the deepest existential commitments pitted against each other . . . where compromise is ruled out on principle."[3] Without necessarily agreeing with Reuther's conclusions, one can agree with her thesis that today's schism is one of faith not just of culture. Today's differences cut across age groups, across such worn out labels as *liberal* and *conservative*. Presently groups are re-aligning themselves along new and sharper divisions.

What is needed today, it seems, is witness to a pluralism that will be rich enough to allow for differences and loving enough to live in peace with these differences. What a tremendous opportunity for the religious community in an age of struggling ecumenism, widening generation gap, and explosive racial conflict.

Experimenting with small groups composed of people with shared philosophies of community is one service that the religious congregation can give to the wider world community. Another service might be experimentation with a still wider, more embracing pluralism. Religious communities have already shown that people can live together in peace despite the fact that they come from widely different ethnic groups and economic backgrounds. Even educational differences have been reconciled in terms of a common service to which each person contributes the fullness of his talents. Other forms of pluralism wait the creativity of further experimentation. For instance, there is much talk today of religious and laity working together. Could this be done in the context of the same community, not with the laity as members of a "third order" but as part of the same congregation, equal in every way? Or, more daring still, could there be a congregation where some members respond in marriage while others answer the call to celibacy, but all are bound by the same beliefs?

Ecumenical communities are already in existence, where members of differing religious groups live together, bound by their faith in Jesus Christ and their common salvation in him. Another area where some progress has been made is that of racially mixed communities. Though all congregations are open to members of all races, still the percentages of blacks and of orientals remain very small. This is a question of particular concern for missionary congregations that have great need to incarnate their communities in the world they wish to serve.

A final suggestion might be the incorporation of persons who have already lived through one career and now are ready for a second. Widows and widowers, for example, have always been "admitted to religious congregations," but the very procedures which "allowed" them to enter were almost insuperable barriers for most of them. Today there seem to be new possibilities for mature persons, already formed professionally, to follow an individual program of incorporation into the community.

In all these and many other ways, pluralism can be expressed in religious communities today. That such pluralism is part of what it means to be community is one of the conclusions of the Taizé group: "The ecumenical vocation is not different from that of being called to religious community."[4]

6 / Communities in change

*Ordinarily, there is nothing so hard for the religious
man to cope with as social change. He feels
threatened and his instant reaction is defensive and
abusive. Historically, he has some reason to feel
this way. Massive social change inevitably affects
the religious life of society.*
DANIEL CALLAHAN, *"Toward a Theology of Secularity"**

FOR THE religious man, change is always a difficulty and even a
threat, and the current upheaval in church and religious congregation makes change seem more ominous. The issues are no longer just
the practical aspects of what to change and when. The question is
rather one of the whole meaning and value of change and its implications for forming community.

What does it mean to change? To go from what-is-not-yet to what-
may-be. Change is becoming; it is growth; it is movement toward
the future. But it is also a leaving behind, a setting off, a going beyond. These are the polarities of change and something of its ten-
sions. Change is a human category, for man alone of all the animals
is fully perceptive of change; only he can make his past part of his
present; only he can draw the future into the here and now. Anxiety
and guilt are human concerns, as are anticipation and forgiveness.

Man is not only the object of change; he is also its subject. In
short man is responsible for change, both in himself and in his
world. As Teilhard de Chardin has phrased it, "Man is evolution

The Secular City Debate (New York: Macmillan, 1966), p. 91.

becoming conscious of itself." Today man is almost self-consciously aware that he is responsible for something that has grown beyond his easy control. At times, he wants to shout out, in the words of the popular expression, "Stop the world and let me get off." But the reality of change in the world cannot be stopped, cannot even be slowed down. Man cannot get off; or, at best, he attempts to do so at his own peril, for change is real and an unwillingness to face its reality can only be a symptom of neurosis. We say that the rigid person is ill, or at least, tending toward illness, while the adjusted person is one who can bend without breaking. On the other hand, we classify the person who changes with every shifting wind as unstable and fickle. Somewhere in between the all inclusive "Everything is always changing," and the equally absolute, "Nothing changes," there must be a balance. On the one hand, man receives his reality in a constant succession of "nows." On the other hand, there is something in man that reaches out to permanence, that wants the security of what is stable. The danger is that man so easily confuses what is passing with what is permanent, or makes the timeless into the transitory.

What is timeless and unchanging in man? Robert Johann has answered that it is his selfhood,

> His awareness of other persons and his permanent vocation to promote their welfare. It is his freedom to change his mind, to regret his past and mend his ways. The timeless in man is his openness to the Infinite, which prevents anything yet accomplished from becoming the final word. With the Absolute for his horizon, his future dwarfs his past, and what he has is nothing compared with what is still being done.[1]

Paradoxically enough, what is changeless in man is his unending capacity for change. To be open to truth, I must be willing to change my mind. To be willing to adapt, I must be free enough to let go of comfortable ways of doing things. In short, I must be willing to grow.

At first glance, it would seem that "man's unchanging capacity for change" is greatest in the young and malleable, and from the standpoint of physical adaptibility this is certainly true. But the more profound human changes come only with increasing maturity, for only the maturing person can choose with growing self-realization and freedom from compulsion. Even the willingness to change, which is the fundamental attitude behind that prized contemporary virtue of adaptability, presupposes a growing experience of the need to change. In the same way, patience with change comes only through repeated failures to stabilize patterns of action. Such patience is an essential part of being mature enough to accept the human condition, a gradual growth that takes time. Christian maturing is also built on this capacity for change, the willingness to convert from old ways to new ways. This capacity of the Christian for change includes, not only his desire to "throw off the old man," but even more profoundly, his acceptance of Christ's saving action, of being transformed into Christ.

Resistance to change

Given this capacity for change as *the* unchanging element in human and Christian maturation, the question may well be asked, why does man find change so difficult?

One of the strongest cases for the position of the "immobilists" was delineated by the evolutionist, Teilhard de Chardin, when he wrote,

> the immobilists have common sense on their side, habit of thought, inertia, pessimism and also, to some extent, morality and religion. . . . For the sake of human tranquility, in the name of and in defense of the sacred established Order, the immobilists forbid the earth to move. Nothing changes, they say, or can change.[2]

So man attempts to justify his resistance to change in terms of common sense, of habit, even of the sacredness of moral and religious values. Yet many of the reasons for reluctance to change lie still deeper in the psyche of man. Perhaps one reason why man hesitates to accept change is the realization that ultimately any change will call for change in himself. It is so easy to identify the static with the secure, not realizing that lack of flexibility is in direct opposition to safety.

The Christian also finds himself heir to a long tradition that tends to identify perfection with what is immutable. God's perfection is seen as Absolute and unchanging. Tradition implies a judging of the present in terms of what has been valid in the past. But this is to deny that continuity means continuing action. Those traditionalists who seek to identify tradition with the past fail to realize that, in its truest sense, "tradition comes from the past, but looks forward into the future." In this way it "always tried to answer current problems; it grows and renews itself."[3]

To be a true traditionalist means, then, to be willing to move beyond one's present position. But the fearful question remains: Where will we go; into what strange country are we moving? It is so much more comfortable to settle down, to hope that threatening change will not uproot us. So resistance to change is linked with fear of the future. It takes a searching look at one's own defenses to realize that such fear is fundamentally unchristian. For the Christian is always in pilgrimage, moving from his present position and journeying into a strange country. As Harvey Cox has reminded us, Scripture describes the sinner as the one who is lame and deaf, asleep and even dead, all of which are images of immobility. It is from such static and closed-in positions that the sinner must be converted, if he is to *live*.[4]

One reason why a man is so resistant to this call to transcendence is his lack of trust and belief. What will tomorrow bring? At times all a man can do is to wait and to watch. The changes he desires come too slowly; the changes he fears are already upon him. He can neither hurry the one nor delay the other. He lives in expectation— and what could be more Christian!

Such a summons to live in hope of what is to come is one of the positive values of change in a rapidly evolving world. When a man is secure and settled, his world tends to shrink to the size of himself. When things are constantly changing, the world eludes man's grasp and stretches out, open, ever widening. Such a man lives in expectation walking on the knife edge between despair and hope. He lives dangerously but he lives like a man. He also lives like a Christian. Constant change prevents him from yielding to the temptation of making false gods out of past practices. Like the Jews of old, contemporary man is still making golden calves, not as outright idols but rather to concretize God, making him in man's image and likeness. By stabilizing religion men seek security, limiting God to what is familiar.

But constant change calls a man to detachment from the securities of both past and present practice. Such detachment, such wandering in the desert of insecurity can enable a man to experience what his intellect readily admits, that he is not absolute master of his life and his actions. Periods of change detach a man from the safety of the past and teach him to trust in what is to come. Still, both these attitudes have an element of negation. The past is finished; the future is not yet. Only the present offers itself to man. Such is the *kairos* of the Bible where the present situation, the present moment, the present opportunity, contains both the past and the future. It is to the present that man brings the past; it is in the present that his future begins to take shape.

The present, then, is the moment of change and decision. Here a man says his creative "Yes" or "No" and so makes his world. Responsibility for present change is one of man's reasons for clinging to the past. No man likes to be uprooted, and yet the Christian is one who experiences constant conversion from past faults and failings, accompanied by a willingness to assume the responsibilities of a free man. A Christian is one who is radically open to God and this is to be ready to concur with him in converting, changing the world.

Such are a few reasons why man finds change so difficult: the security of the static; resistance to conversion that causes a man to harden in his present ways; the special aura surrounding tradition that has become identified with "the way things have always been done." Fear of the unknown, uncertainty of the individual concerning his own ability to adapt to the new are some of man's commonsense reasons for resisting changing.

Overcoming resistance to change

Writing on the brighter side of man's state of constant change, Robert Johann points out that:

> The contemporary breakdown of habits forces man to reassess his ways, to recognize the limitations inherent in current procedures. He is called once more to situate his large-scale behavior in the context of the Eternal and try to make it less inadequate to the full range of his possibilities. By compelling him to take a stand on issues he would otherwise have neglected, the collapse of habit makes possible a wider, richer achievement. In short, only the discomfort of crisis keeps habit from becoming a rut and the eternal in man from going completely to sleep.[5]

But even when this theoretical value of change is admitted, resistance on the practical level remains. Resistance can be lessened somewhat by a deep respect for the sincerity of those who find themselves threatened by change. For each of us knows from our own experience that the sharp stone of criticism and the hard edge of argument, all too often leave us unconvinced. We need understanding more than we need convincing. Such acceptance and honest admission of fear of change is the beginning of the gradual decline of that same fear.

Another way to lessen fear of change is to diminish the threat it poses to a man's self-identity. One way to do this is to provide a generous margin for mistakes. Both those who are initiating change and those who are trying to live in a world made less secure by constant change need to know that infallibility is not a human virtue. There is a great deal of psychological security in constantly reminding oneself that mistakes are a part of healthy living, and that the greater and more rapid the changes, the greater must be a man's patience with his own and his neighbor's failures.

The recognition of levels of change may also eliminate some of the confusion about the difficulties of change. To change things is relatively easy; to change behavior comes a bit harder. But to change attitudes presents the greatest difficulty. Obviously, every change involves something of all three. Unfortunately arguments about the pros and cons of change tend to settle down to the level of things to be changed, leaving the attitudes of those who resist untouched. As a consequence the real value, or lack of it, in the proposed change is ignored, and the discussion ends in useless bickering. Perhaps change in behavior is the mediating point in transmitting the value of change. The experience of behaving in a different way can bring about a gradual change in attitude and finally the acceptance of new ways of doing things.

Since many of those who resist change do so in the name of tradition and authority, it follows that authority has a key role to play in making change acceptable. If those in authority are themselves able to accept change as a value, they can do much to make it less threatening. They can also initiate changes, control the rate of change, provide examples of successful change.

Change can also be made more acceptable if the new is linked with the old, not by slogans and specious claims but by a genuine attempt to show that what is proposed as new has really grown out of the old. New values transcend what has gone before, but to transcend is not to deny. Rather it is to catch up and continue the former, to fulfill what is promised, to move closer to what the past hoped to achieve. Such an attitude toward change stresses a dynamic continuity of the old finding itself in the new, with the new, in its turn, giving way to still further changes so that man may grow into the future.

Finally, the whole area of trust needs re-emphasis if change is to promote unity and not fracture it in useless argumentation. Basic is that trust which respects every man's truth, whether he resist change or actively promote it. Both positions are necessary if there is to be balance between too much change and too little. Along with this trust in each other, men need to trust in a future that is and will be given to them. Together we need to say, "I believe in tomorrow."

Community and change

In all of the above the emphasis has been on change as basically human, as essentially Christian. To be a person is to be for and with others; to be a Christian is to be incorporated into a community that is being redeemed. So change is not just a matter for individuals; it is also communitarian. Such a statement seems something of a truism; but the renewal of the seventies is placing new emphasis on community and change and the relationship between change in the individual and change in the group.

First of all, since community is built on the response of persons, one to another, it is built on a principle of dynamism. Since people change in themselves and in their relationships with each other, communities must be open and flexible. Since the needs of persons change, the community has to be sensitive in its response to these needs.

Change is also an area where members of the community can be of great help to each other. Just as a man cannot be joyful by himself, so too he cannot change by himself. He needs another to point out his need to change, to summon him to change. He needs others to support him in the insecurities of change. And he also needs those others whose initial resistance to change will cause him to face responsibly the meaning of change. Both the individual who promotes change, as well as the one who resists it, must see what change will mean, not just for himself, but also for the community. Will this particular change build the community, helping to break down those barriers which separate individuals from one another, which isolate one religious community from the wider communities of church and world?

If change is to promote community, keep it open and flexible, then it must come from the community, involve the members of the community and, finally, be evaluated by them. In this way change will form the community, reform it, reflect its growth.

Individuals who participate in community change will, in general, find less difficulty in adopting the new forms. They will be more likely to understand the reasons for change. The potential resister will also be reassured when he sees that the values of the group are also changing. Since most people tend to identify with the group and group standards, "resistance to change lies in the relation of the individual to the values of his group."[6] But if the values of the group reflect openness to proposed change, then individual members are reassured; they feel accepted when and if they change.

To effect change in a community it is not enough simply to involve the members, since to change a community means, ultimately, to change an institution. This gives rise to another whole set of problems. Since "every community endeavors to become an institution in order to provide external form for itself and to ensure its continuity, change in the institution threatens community identity."[7] Yet in a truer sense, change preserves community by providing for its continuity, opening it to the future. Still the very largeness of the institution, the somewhat permanent character of its structure, all make institutional change a slow business. In the sharp criticism of Abbé Houtart, institutions "will always be a little late with the facts."[8]

One of the burning questions in religious communities today is how "little" and how "late" and still survive? Institutions seem fated to lag behind the drive of their more forward looking members. This is a safety element, giving the institution a better chance to survive. It is also a danger, creating a tension that may reach a destructive level. In periods of rapid change, this institutional lag becomes even more apparent and the agony more real.

Since the fundamental issue is one of community, the rate of change in the group cannot be slowed down to the pace of those who are most resistant to change; on the other hand, it cannot be so accelerated that the majority are left bewildered. If only those who wish for more rapid change could accept a measure of restraint in the form of patient love; if only those who were more reluctant to change could begin to move in the name of conversion, change might unify community.

In a similar way, loyalty to the institutional character of the community seems to require that members remain within the institution, rather than abandon it to slow deterioration. Change can only come from within. As Roger Schutz points out, "To consent to the Church's institutions, to become solidary with them, is to become really able to be the ferment in the dough. When a leaven is truly a ferment, what a power does it possess to raise the dough and to burst open the crust that constantly forms again on aging institutions."[9]

The questions of how rapidly a community should change, and of the whole area of loyalty to slowly changing institutions, are delicate matters calling for the honest decision of individuals and the concern of the total community. It would seem, however, that if a decision has to be made about the pace of renewal, it must be made in favor of the future. It is the young who will be formed by change or deformed by failure to change. Presumably the more mature, more stable members of the community will be less affected by rate and kind of change. Hopefully, such members are less concerned for personal security and more committed to the continuity of community.

As long as an individual can live in community, keeping alive his hope in its future, working for its growth and development, then neither his loyalty nor his membership are in question. But if a member really "loses hope" in his community's capacity for renewal; if he finds that his own potential to live in such a community is so restricted, then he is no longer able to work for change, and he has already left the community. Perhaps the more honest thing for him is to leave the institution. These are hard words. They are critical words. It is to be hoped that every-time a member leaves a community, it will be an occasion for that community to "reform" itself, to re-examine its capacity to meet changing needs, both in individuals and in the world.

In theory, at least, religious communities should be in the vanguard of change, "flexible and ahead of the rest, for the benefit of the church."[18] Such is the ideal position of the religious community examining its attitude toward change. On the one hand, religious congregations have a past that makes them part of the dynamic tradition of the church. They also have an eschatological dimension that keeps them open to what lies ahead. As the Rule of Taizé phrases it, "standing still is disobedience for Brothers advancing towards Christ."

But in the practical order, religious communities have been notoriously slow to change. This is due, partly, to the sacralization of permanence that has affected the whole church, and partly to the detailed directives and large doses of routine that have allowed religious to "settle down." Habitual ways of acting have been sanctified, and any attempt to break these patterns could only be met with suspicion. Those who advocated change were image breakers, shattering the identity of community, and threatening techniques of salvation. Such conservatism is most understandable in the light of past value systems, but the truth of the matter is that religious communities must become centers of experimentation, signs of progress in church and world. If, in the past, religious have been symbols of stability, today they must stand for the flexible and the open.

Part of the service that religious communities can give to a changing world is to reiterate the priority of person over law, of community over institution. They can show concern for the strain that change brings to individuals and for the dangers of eroding values and consequent apathy and anomie. Out of their own experience religious communities can speak of ways of relieving these strains and eliminating these dangers. Periods of rapid change demonstrate the pointlessness of many of today's new forms which seem more like symptoms of restlessness rather than signs of progress. Change that is also development is motivated by desire for personal growth, insight into new apostolic needs, opportunities for fuller service. Change is for the sake of persons and communities; it is not change for the sake of change.

Another service that religious communities can give to the world is a Christian witness to the poverty required by constant change. To change is not easy, but it is human; it is gospel; it is creative. Hopefully something of this creativity will be captured in the religious rules now beginning to be formulated. In place of detailed directives the rule of the future "will be the love of Christ as he presents himself in his members to be served. The security of system and pattern will be replaced by courage and trust and realistic love."[11] Such an ideal will have to be lived, not just spoken if it is to become a reality. Religious communities who believe in this kind of personal responsibility, who live in such trust, can demonstrate that such flexibility is possible.

Finally, religious communities can become specialists in change "in education, in social work, in the liturgical movement, the catechetical movement, in all the specialized fields of action where we need people exclusively devoted to study, to research, to thought, to experimentation in order to perform the task of theological adaptation and continuing renewal."[12] In this way religious can contribute to a badly needed philosophy of change. They can remain open to God's continuing action, reflect on it as a community, and make their experience available to the whole Christian community. They can admit mistakes, seek new directions, respond to present needs. In short they can change what needs changing, while preserving the best of the "traditional" past. Such religious communities will realize the ideal sketched by Cardinal Newman as an old man of seventy-seven writing to his fellow Oratorians. "Our congregation is now entering on its normal state. To be ever one and the same, to be ever changing, both together, one as much as the other is its normal state . . . henceforth, change is an element of our existence."[13]

7 / Community as task-oriented

If you live alone, whose feet will you wash?
ST. BASIL THE GREAT

PERHAPS ONE of the first questions any community in process of renewal should ask is: "What is this community for? For itself, for the growth of its members? Or is it for other, for the wider community of world and church?" One of the tragedies of the past that still haunts our questioning today is the implied dichotomy built into the question itself, the either/or. Either a community turned in on itself, or a community going out to others. Phrased in this bold fashion, community and apostolate can only turn out to be contradictories and, in the practical order, this has often happened.

There are those who feel that building community takes priority. Time spent together, communal prayer, dialogue and discussion within the community come first. These, and other community exercises, are absolutely necessary if the members are to serve the wider community effectively. Others give priority to community "for others," stressing that a community comes together in order to serve. Priority must be given to the needs of the apostolate, and community itself is built in terms of unity in service.

In a sense, both positions are in fundamental agreement; both value community building; both stress service. Conflict comes in terms of the pragmatic "how." How much emphasis should be put on building a strong internal community so that the members can really be messengers of the good news? How much response should be made to the demands of an apostolate that implies sacrifice of present being-together so that the community can open itself more completely to the needs of the wider community? These are the questions being raised very pragmatically in this period of renewal. New life-forms are being created: what shape will they take? Certainly they will be formative of apostolic communities. But what meaning will be given to this very traditional phrase?

Negatively, it seems safe to say that in the immediate future communities will no longer describe themselves in terms of some one particular work, designated as their secondary purpose for being a community. In a sense this development simply recognizes a situation of fact. Communities which originated in order to "serve the sick poor," "to provide schools for the indigent," or "to educate young ladies in higher schools," have long since branched out into all kinds of other apostolic works. But to say that communities will no longer have a single apostolic work as their secondary purpose is to say much more than just positing a wider spread of activities. It is also to deny that apostolate is, in any sense, secondary. It is also to shift the word *apostolic* from work to person. Since both of these points have already been elaborated upon, they will simply be noted here. It is more to our purpose in this chapter to investigate the meaning of apostolic community. What follows are a few suggestions as to such meaning in terms of: the language of action, the forming of community through task, and a few practical applications of task in relation to community.

Language of action

No community has meaning in itself; its meaning is in terms of others. To be human is to be related to others. All religious communities are identified in terms of service, and any distinction of contemplative communities versus apostolic communities tends to mislead by setting up contraries where there should be complementaries. Every community must be open and outgoing, at the service of others, and so, apostolic.

To put it in another way, every community must speak, must have something to say, otherwise it has no reason for being. Like the persons who compose it, every community is a word; it expresses something, says something unique and unrepeatable. It has its own meaning, a meaning which is expressed both in its prayer and in its service. It has a different meaning at different times and to different people. All of which reiterates the commonly acknowledged fact that communication is at the heart of community. No community can be formed without communication and, in a sense, there can be no communication without some community. In any case, this need for communication immediately calls to mind such verbalizations as dialogue and discussion. It also points toward a language of action.

"Actions speak louder than words" is one of those proverbial statements usually used to moralize about the power of good example. But it can also be an expression of something much deeper. Actions are words and, as such, they too form community, and community, in turn, is formed by what it does. To live together in community is to say something; it is also to do something and so to be a bearer of the good news, a messenger, an apostle. But it is also true that part of what forms the community originally is the language of common action, common purpose. It is in this sense that a forming community, a re-forming community needs not only to discuss its goals and purposes but also to do something together, to discover themselves in their communal apostolic action.

But before this discussion goes any further, perhaps there is need to clarify the meaning of doing things together. In the past, this has usually meant working side by side, or at least being engaged in a comparable apostolate, for example teaching in elementary schools or working in hospitals.

Today's shift of "apostolic" from work to person allows for a much more fluid meaning of "working together." In a recent article on "Formation and Task," Vincent Branick points out that the objective of a community is not work, but goal or task. He goes on to explain that:

> Task is the creation of values that can be shared, values not simply of an individual subject but of a public world, where many can partake. Yet, task is more than a man's material work. It includes also his duty of worship of God, his duty to be thoughtful and thankful of truth and beauty, because such duties are eminently public, even when accomplished in silence. Task is the outward-going service of that which is not self.[1]

Task, then, is the expression of a personal community; it is the sharing and expression of values—not just individual values, but public values. Task is creative and so is personal. In contrast, organization and getting the job done are the work of functional societies. In such societies the relationships of the members are business-like; they are based on getting the work accomplished. Persons are valued in terms of their ability to function in the society. And in many cases persons are seen as replaceable, or at best, interchangeable parts. In short, the relationship of persons in functional societies is external; membership is based on exchange of services and mutuality of interests.

In the community, as it has already been described, the basis for the members being together is their personal relationship to each other: mutual responsibility and solidarity of salvation. In such a relationship each person is unique and irreplaceable. He is valued because of who he is, not because of what he does. Such a relationship, interestingly enough, has an element of disinterestedness in it, at least in the sense that members are not primarily concerned with each other's "market value," how each performs, whether the individual's skill is needed or can be used in the "operation." For in terms of task, each person contributes something to the creative vision and formation of values.

Yet this personal relationship, this creation of values, needs to be embodied in some form of common action, some work. And this brings us back to task and the language of action. Common purpose both expresses community and also forms it. For the present, let us concentrate on the former and then return to the latter.

In the excellent article just referred to, Vincent Branick goes on to point out that:

> The convergence of the members with each other results from the convergence of all the members on a common goal. In selfless striving for this goal, the members find themselves united. Their mutual confidence rests on the confidence each has that the other is striving for the community goal, or at least is not surreptitiously seeking his personal advantage to the detriment of that goal.[2]

In this way, service to others expresses community because in the freedom of give and take in community, it finds the practical day to day expression of growing in that love which is at the heart of all community. Service also provides a realistic expression of that trust in others which is so fundamental to any real living together.

By way of contrast again, organizational structure, work, can be divided up. Each person can be given responsibility for a specific job and held accountable for its completion. Failure to do the job is soon apparent, and a man is warned to improve or to leave. But once the assigned job is done, an individual's responsibility ends; he "goes home," lives his own life in the life community to which he belongs.

But in terms of community task, the question is entirely different. The task is too big for any one man; so a community is formed. In a sense, task is too big for any community; it can never be "finished," can never be called completed. Task transcends community in much the same way that community and the persons who form it, by their very nature, are transcendent. A person does not find his meaning primarily in himself, but rather in his relationship to others. A community does not find its identity solely by concentrating on itself, but by going out to others in service. Each personal relationship opens the way to further relationships. Each opening of the community calls for still greater openness. Every task of the Christian calls a man to go beyond himself, challenges the community to deeper involvement, invites it to assume still more responsibility for still greater tasks.

But task also limits community. In fact, it is a very real expression of the limits of both man and community; it is a concrete realization of the human paradox of man called both to transcend himself and to be a finite creature, loved in his very limitedness. Just as a man discovers himself in his relationship with others, so too he discovers his own limitations in these same relationships. He can only relate to a circumscribed number of people, and even the deepest of these relationships still has inherent limitations. These limitations are not just boundaries of his own choosing; they are also expressions of the kind of man he is. In a similar way, task limits community; a community can only do so much, give expression to certain values. But in this expression it finds its own identity, direction and unification. Task expresses the character and spirit of a congregation.

It is one of the difficulties of present renewal that as congregations seek to discover and express their own identity and to find their way through the bewilderments of this last half of the twentieth century, they are turning in more and more on themselves and in so doing are losing the very perspective that is theirs as task-oriented communities.

Certainly some of this is reaction to the functionary status found in so many religious congregations in the immediate past. Without laboring the point, it cannot be denied that religious communities have tended to identify themselves with the doing of certain works. They have tended to organize themselves like societies whose function was to get the job done; persons were replaceable; their value and identity tied up with their capacity to perform certain needed works.

But, as we have seen, task is not just a job to be done; it is a goal, a unifying purpose. It is a response of a community to make the world more human, more Christian, more ready for Christ's coming. Each man is called to take part in this task; he gives expression to his willingness to participate by doing certain works. But these works may change; they can be modified in terms of individual talent and greater community need. What remains permanent is the vision of person and community as to what is of value. One of the challenges of task as expressive of community is that of recognition. The question, "What needs to be done?" can only be answered in terms of function, and the answer often appears before the questioner has even punctuated his sentence. But task must be discovered. It answers the question, "How can I, how can we, contribute?" a question that is communitarian and that calls for the help of many in searching out an answer.

Ultimately, each man must discover his own task and freely accept that task as his. But if task depends on the responsible acceptance of each man, how can one speak of community task? Only in the sense that a group of individuals discover that they share the same vision, the same values, and wish to assume responsibility for giving creative expression to this vision. In the original formation of religious communities, a group of men who shared a vision came together; their shared vision, to which they wished to give expression, is what brought them together as a community. This vision of the founders arose within the context of a certain situation, and it was in response to this situation that the apostolic works of the community were chosen. So today any return "to the spirit of the founder" must, first of all, take into consideration these specific historical circumstances, attempt to discover the way in which this situation was revelatory of human need and then plan on ways to meet this human need in terms of today's changing circumstances.

It would seem, then, that a religious congregation already bonded by the responsibility of love and service could both find unity and express unity through a kind of communal meditation, a search and discovery of "What are we for today?" This question, with its implied limitations and its built-in transcendence is at the heart of renewal. It reveals the unique identity of the community in a way that no amount of internal self-scrutiny can do.

Forming community through task

Just as task expresses community, presupposes community, it is also true to say that community is formed by task. This can be exemplified very simply in terms of the origins of most religious congregations, where groups of persons saw a specific need, enlarged their vision to see beyond the individual job to be done, and so almost inadvertently became founders of religious communities. It was the shared vision of task that brought this group together, and once together, it was the exigencies of the task that began to shape the community and give it a certain life-style.

Once again, language both expresses a man's thought and also somehow shapes it. German language is different from French or English; Germans think differently from Frenchmen or Englishmen, and part of this difference comes from the formative difference in language. This is one of the reasons why translations always prove inadequate; the language is somehow bound up with the thought, to the extent that certain idioms are almost untranslatable. And the symbolic language of poetry loses its meaning when it is rendered into prose, just as the rigor of logic cannot make sense out of much of contemporary poetry. In a similar way, different generations speak different languages and even though they use the same words, their meaning is poles apart.

Today, religious communities, suffering from the same generation gap that is so apparent in our larger society, find that their members no longer speak the same language, even when they use the same words. Some commentators on religious life seem to suggest that this is a relatively simple problem, just a vocabulary gap, and imply that it could be bridged by some sort of dictionary that would translate "temporary vows" into "a year's commitment," or "striving for perfection" into "personal fulfillment." Though such translations would certainly prove helpful, unless they were accompanied by something more effective in changing thought patterns, it is doubtful whether they would really bridge the gap.

But the language of action may yet prove the most effective translation. Just as strangers who do not share the same native language can still communicate through gestures, so too, engaging in shared task can bind together the members of a whole congregation. For it is in the language of action that a man comes to reflect on what his ideals really are; he expresses these ideals in his work and, at the same time, his work, if it is truly human, raises constant questions as to meaning. "What am I doing?" is a concrete translation of "Who am I?" In a similar way, a community forms itself, takes on a certain identity in terms of task. A community that sees its task as spreading the good news of the gospel becomes evangelical. Or, at least, it discovers in a painfully real way what it means to live a gospel life.

This interrelationship between personal identity and work, which allows both person and community to be expressed in and formed by task, is a particularly human category. Work is not just punishment for sin; it is an opportunity for man to grow and assume his rightful relationship with the world and with other men. In this sense, work is both impersonal and personal. It is impersonal because it allows a man to communicate with other men with a greater degree of objectivity. Work is a "something" and, as such, it allows men to speak through an impersonal medium. But work is also personal, because it is so expressive and formative of the person himself.

Community needs the impersonal language of action, along with the more personal communication of dialogue, to provide a balance between objectivity and subjectivity. Men who share the same task say something to each other in an "a-personal" way that is still expressive of themselves. And this can help to bridge the generation gap where words divide but where there can still be the unity of shared vision.

With present stress on personalism, perhaps there is particular need for calling attention to the less personal language of action. In this way the corporal expression of action can be formative of truly human communities. "Our interpersonal relationships are not simply encounters between spirits. Human community demands the creation of values through corporal work as a medium of communication. Task, as an impersonal category, is an indispensable presupposition for a truly human personalism."[3]

Because task is so important as a medium of communication, it becomes an indispensable part of forming community and so counteracts to a great extent the threat implied in the question of which takes priority: community or apostolate. Rather than two opposing principles, building community within and serving the wider community without become two ways of expressing what it means to be human with other human beings. Perhaps one of the best expressions of this basic unity is that of Eugene Kennedy when he described the "real communities of this world" as "people who love and share a common purpose of giving themselves for the sake of God's people."[4]

Since task becomes such an important factor in forming genuine community, it would seem to follow that one of the most important criteria for those planning to enter community would be their ability to share the communal task, to contribute to that vision by which a community recognizes its own unique task in church and in world. In short, the capacity to form community can be described as the ability to work together with others in giving concrete expression to their unique creative vision.

This willingness to share in the communal task is much more than just an ability to work with others in order to get the job done. It lies in a deeper commitment to seeking out the will of God together, contributing to this on-going search, accepting that this task is never completed but is constant invitation. Forming an apostolic community means being willing to support others in their task, being open, in turn, to receiving support from others and simple enough even to ask for it. It means being obedient, first of all to the Spirit speaking in every other member, speaking also in that most unlikely person of all, oneself. It means allowing oneself to be formed by the exigencies of the communal task, the unique mission of the particular community that is being formed.

Finally, if task is formative of community, as well as expressive of it, then community structures, discussed in a previous chapter, must also be shaped by and be expressive of the community's task. Surely one of the most daring concepts found in the "Decree on the Renewal and Adaptation of Religious Life" is that apostolic service is of the very essence of religious life.

Everything else in religious life can be structured in subordination to this service. Such an orientation will prevent religious communities from becoming so absorbed in the details of their own internal ordering that they become too self-conscious to be of much service at all. As Eugene Kennedy has forcefully suggested:

> It is time for renewal to let all the arguments about revised schedules and reformed habits fall aside, so that seminarians, priests, and religious can confront the basic issues which must be understood if they are to fulfill their vocations of service. The fundamental issue is to understand the meaning of the Church and its ministry to the human race. Singularly enough, we have given very little time to the discussion of this basic, if difficult, question.[5]

Applications of task to community

Beginning with the question of tension between community and apostolate, this chapter has moved into a consideration of task as the permanent vision of values which a community both expresses and makes effective. Furthermore, this communal task forms the community itself, giving it a kind of unity and uniqueness. All of this means that apostolic community is not an organization for getting jobs done, even jobs that badly need to be done. It is not a source of cheap labor, making it possible for the church to provide certain specific kinds of services. A community forms and is formed by an ideal concretized in response to task.

What task? First and foremost the task of any community is to be community, to accept, to recognize, to live out the implications that men are brothers, that Christians are those who dare to sing *"Our* Father," to commit themselves to gospel living. Above all, they are called to give expression to the good news that someday "all men will be one." As the "Decree on the Renewal and Adaptation of Religious Life" points out, community itself has "great apostolic influence . . . for such brotherly unity shows that Christ has come" (no. 15). To grow in unity in community, then, is to grow in service. But to be unified in service is no easy task.

Just as common vision unifies community and gives its communal vision substance, so too, a lack of such common vision destroys community and, consequently, militates against its real service to the church.

> Where members disagree on the basic task of the community, where they dispute the primary purpose of themselves as a group, there can be no dynamic coherence. No amount of dedication of the members to each other as individuals can supply for this lack of dedication to a common task. No matter how much the members love one another as persons, they cannot function together. That is, accord can exist between individuals, but not between members of a functioning community.[6]

This is not to suggest, however, that all the members of a community must agree on one, best way of fulfilling their common task. Here diversity of means seems part of the essential unity of the group, pluralism part of the richness a community brings to the accomplishment of its task.

What does seem important is the focus of a religious congregation on the fundamental question: "What are we for?" To be honest, this question must be faced in full freedom, including freedom from any preconceived prejudice in favor of certain job commitments currently binding the congregation. It must also include the free recognition that raising such a basic issue risks dividing the congregation. For instance, one part of the group may feel that its fundamental task is the preservation of traditional values; another group may see its task in terms of commitment to immediate human needs wherever they are to be found; and still others may feel called to the task of living a very fluid and mobile life, expressive of the church's role of revealing the future to mankind. All of these are creative visions, capable of calling communities into being, but they do not form a single task, uniting one community. Different communities, formed by these different visions, might all do the same kind of work, but their tasks that form them into communities would be radically different.

Despite such risks of discovering division, the question of task is at the heart of community renewal. This question cannot be answered simply by making evaluations of present apostolic works, though such evaluations may be very necessary. This question of task calls for a broader consideration of world and church that goes beyond the personnel resources of the congregation and past expressions of secondary purpose, and is formative of communities for the future.

Another application of task as formative and expressive of community is the re-evaluation of certain talents as fitting persons for certain congregations. Each person is a unique gift to community for he brings his own unique person to the community which he helps to form. His gift, his talents can find expression in the creative vision of any community. The question no longer is: Can this person's talents be used in the specific work done by this congregation? but rather: Can this person share in the community's task by sharing in its creation of values? Diversity of gifts is essential to the fulfilling of communal task, since creative vision means multiple expression and pluralism of means. Task creates community by allowing the members to complement each other, while they join in accomplishing what all agree is worth doing.

As members of religious congregations move from one job

to another, as they find themselves no longer able to "stay on the job," they simply take on new ways of expressing, fulfilling the task of the community. At a time when religious congregations enter more realistically into competitive, functional societies, their members need to know that competition is on the level of society and not on the level of community. Even when they can no longer function in society, they are still vital to community task.

One final caution. To ask religious congregations to focus renewal on the question of "What are we for?" is not to suggest that after a suitable period of reflection, chapter deliberation, and writing of directives, a community should be able to come up with a clear and unequivocal answer about just what its task is. We do not expect individuals, or even ourselves, to be so definite about their own identity. Nor can we expect this of a religious community. As Moran points out:

> The specific work (task) of the congregation may never be more than hazily defined. This does not mean that the people in it do not know what they are about. Most people are not very adept at defining what it means to be human, but they recognize some things that seem to contribute to the human and other things which are certainly opposed to it.[7]

Similarly, a man may know that certain actions are expressive of himself while others are destructive of himself. A community must also come to share its insights about what is constructive and destructive of its fundamental task. The ways in which this task will be met will always be changing means.

To renew an apostolic community is to recognize that the present works of the community are changing, that they may or may not be expressive of the task of the community. It is to allow task to structure community and not to force the creative vision of new tasks into the old wine skin of inflexible structures. All of this is in order to allow community to grow and form itself anew through the creative dialectic of assembly together and missioning forth in service of others.

8 / Community and suffering

Man is not merely an individual nature looking for its own fulfillment; he is a person summoned by love. He is called not to comfort but to creativity; not to satisfaction, but to service. The price of such service runs high; it involves even death. But the stakes are higher still—they involve God himself.

ROBERT JOHANN, *"Beyond Grief"**

MAN IS MADE for heaven, so it seems rather natural that he tends to lean forward, to expect, rather unrealistically, that he can live heaven now. And certainly there is an element of underlying truth in this apparent naïveté. Man has been redeemed; he can rightfully live in a spirit of expectation. Heaven is open; the Christian has every right to rejoice. But it is also true that heaven is not-yet. Man is still being redeemed, and every individual is just beginning to discover the good news; he is still learning to be grateful.

Something of the naïveté that somehow expects to find heaven here and now, somewhere, with some certain group of persons, seems one of the vocational hazards of the religious man. How many Christians "leave the church" because they discover that it is a church of sinners. How many seminarians and young religious give up because they find the professional and professed religious man still imperfect? How many communities are being shaken to their founda-

*America 112 (Jan. 16, 1965), 76.

tions as they face up to the crisis, not only of renewal, but also of reform?

Certainly the whole concept of community has suffered from the unrealistic idealism of many who attempt to describe it. Religious listen to glowing descriptions of how community is essentially a group of persons bound together by love; they read of "shared responsibility," of "creative vision," and then they go back to their own local communities and almost despair. They conclude, too quickly, that community is not possible, given their particular situation, the people with whom they live, the inherent restrictions they face, the resistance to change they find in themselves and in others. And yet, it is here that community will be built, if it is ever going to come into being. For it is man-who-is-still-being redeemed who is being readied for community. Heaven is not-yet; perfect community is not-yet. But it will be! This is the joyous expectation of the Christian that must find the beginnings of its realization in this present pilgrimage.

Since suffering is such an integral part of every man's life, since it is essential to the Christian's sharing in the death-resurrection of Jesus Christ, it follows that suffering will form a necessary part of community; that suffering can be formative of community.

Suffering in community

Perhaps one of the first things that needs to be realized is that suffering is implied in the very notion of person community. This statement is not meant to ignore those sufferings that are part of each individual's life: illness, loss of relatives and friends, fears and insecurities that are part of man's original inheritance. Nor is it intended to minimize those sufferings implied in life communities, or in societies. It simply indicates that the very notion of person community, along with its emphasis on such positive realities as brotherly love, shared responsibility, and creative vision, includes a willingness to be hurt, to share suffering, for communication and dialogue include forgiveness and fraternal correction. Finally, community admits of loneliness and of even greater personal suffering.

To enter into community is to express a certain willingness to allow oneself to be formed in close contact with others, and this is to allow oneself to be hurt. To stay in community requires a capacity, not only to be open enough to admit pain but also to possess a certain capacity for quick healing.

People living closely together in any way are bound to rub edges. When a community is formed on the basic principle of persons responding to each other in truth and freedom there is bound to be friction as persons rub against each other. Such friction cannot be ignored; it must be faced.

In contrast to a society, where a person finds expression and fulfillment for some of his needs, in person community the members are bound together by the whole of their lives in love and mutual responsibility. Whatever concerns one, concerns the whole group. In a society, personality differences, hurt feelings, and jealousies can often be "managed." As long as the persons involved work together in a satisfactory way, there is no real problem. Sometimes successful business partners deliberately live their personal and family lives at a certain distance. They will say: "We work well together and that is as far as we want it to go." And this is as far as it has to go. Only when personal difficulties threaten business relationships must some action be taken, and even then efforts will be made to avoid any confrontation: change in job techniques, rotation of duties and similar manipulations will be tried. Since religious communities also have something of the status of functionary societies, such techniques are not to be despised. But on the other hand, they are not really builders of person community. At best they can be transitional measures, allowing a person to retreat from a situation, to regroup his forces and eventually to face the difficulty with greater personal strength.

Differences between persons in community must ultimately be faced if persons are to grow, if community is ever to "happen." To be a person is to reveal oneself; to be a member of a person community is to participate in shared revelation. It is to meet other persons where they are and this is often in pain. It is to be open to their pain, to share in it, to be willing to be hurt oneself.

To reveal oneself is to open oneself to others. To be honest is to accept the honesty of others. And all of this is to enter ever more deeply into the suffering of person community. To be open to another is to be sensitive to his pain, to suffer with him, to be willing to share his grief, his despair, his walk in the dark. It is to love the honesty of the self he reveals, to see beauty behind the tear-streaked face, the voice that cracks with strain, the body that is tight with struggle.

To accept another's grief, at a time when one's own heart is full is to listen and be open to agony that is expressed in raw and real ways. To accept the revelation of another is to hear what he says, even when his expression is edged with bitterness and violence. It is to be honest enough to believe in another's honesty. And this is to open the way to even more pain.

Today a great deal is said about the need for being honest with each other. But sometimes it sounds as though honesty were a one-way street, where someone had his say while the others listened. But this is only a partial description that reveals very little of the pain and labor involved in such self-revelation. To express a real problem, to share one's suffering, is to risk being misunderstood, to face the possibility that others may fail to recognize the problem, may respond with indifference, perhaps even with laughter. It is to risk even greater pain. It may mean opening oneself to an expression of care and concern that is painful in itself. For instance, to reveal a problem honestly is to face an equally honest question that may call for still deeper self-revelation. It may also result in the free honesty of love which says, "*You* are the problem." Such is the risk and labor of being oneself with others in personal community. At times the price may seem too high.

Such willingness to be hurt is a fundamental down payment on the possibility of community. But the alternative is even more costly. For the only alternative to being oneself, to revealing oneself, is to wear a mask, to keep others at a "proper" distance, to live side by side but not together. It is to let others see only that side of us that we wish to present, rather like a moon, which keeps the same side toward the sun and so is either too hot or too cold for life. As people come to reveal themselves and accept the revelation of others, there will be greater danger of conflict. But conflict need not destroy community; it can even be a strong force in creating it, as the showers of April prepare for growth and the sudden storms of summer clear the air and break out a new day.

Community can be realized only if the people in it can be really themselves. At times this will mean getting hurt. As the Velveteen Rabbit described it to the Skin Horse, "by the time you are Real most of your hair has been loved off, and your eyes drop out and you get loose in the joints and very shabby and old."[1]

But hurting oneself and being hurt is still only part of the story. Being hurtful is another aspect of suffering in community. For one of the pains of living in community is the possibility of hurting others, sometimes inadvertently, sometimes necessarily for the sake of an ultimate healing, sometimes just by being the kind of person one is. None of these very real possibilities are pleasant to face; they make living at a safe distance from others look, on the surface, like a better way to build community. But such a community would be superficial and would give persons no opportunity really to relate to each other in depth, to be together in truth and freedom.

Still another aspect of hurting others in community is the acknowledged responsibility that one's own mistakes will somehow involve others. Someone once described the incarnation as Christ's entering into a community of mistake makers. In a similar way, everyone who enters community identifies himself with others who will make mistakes; he admits that he will add his own share to these mistakes affecting the whole community. To accept community, to form it, is to accept mistake making, and mistake makers. This can be a rather frightening thought, but it can also be an even greater source of inspiration.

To enter into community with other mistake makers is to receive promises of support and strength sufficient to risk failure. It is to promise such support to others, to accept some responsibility for their mistakes, not to deny these mistakes or attempt to cover them over but to express willingness somehow to be community with the mistake maker. It is to say: "He is my brother, she is my sister, and therefore these are lovable persons, not only despite their mistakes, but even because their very mistakes are revealing of persons whom I love."

Mistakes call for forgiveness. There is perhaps no greater gift members of person community can give to each other than an acceptance which is totally for-giving. To have the courage to risk mistakes, to have the honesty to admit them is to call for forgiveness. And this forgiveness must, first of all, come from others. But forgiveness does not come easily, especially in community. Forgiveness must come from the heart. It must be a real forgiveness of a mistake that is hurtful to oneself because it has hurt community.

So in person community one can no longer be disinterested, accepting a formal apology without getting personally involved. In community, forgiveness is not only a matter of accepting the mistakes a brother makes; it is accepting a brother who makes mistakes. This is why forgiveness can never be limited. It is acceptance of this person with all those *original* cracks in his being which come from heredity, culture, early environment, as well as those personal faults that are now as much part of a man as his gait or the expression on his face. Forgiving another as God forgives means always accepting another back into communion.

Another part of forgiving is asking to be forgiven, giving another an opportunity to respond as a brother would. It is strange that in a community of sinners, it is so hard to admit that we "belong." Yet each time a man asks forgiveness, he opens himself to the love of his brother and the healing power of acceptive love.

Forgiving and asking forgiveness in community need not always be a matter of words. There are many ways of saying "I'm sorry," and once again, the language of action may include some of the most expressive forms. Any generous gesture that welcomes back a brother says forgiveness; any action that seeks or accepts reconciliation is for-giving. At times it is necessary to express forgiveness verbally. A member of the community who can freely and simply admit his mistake in the presence of his brothers gives them an opportunity to grow in understanding, both of him and of themselves. He gives them courage to admit their own mistakes and so helps all to enter more fully into the community of sinners which is what every human community must come to see as the truth of itself.

In such asking for forgiveness, the religious man who is on his way to becoming Christian finds that one of the hardest things he is asked to do is to forgive his own weakness. To be generous and pardon others is one thing; to forgive oneself calls for a still deeper sort of love that can rejoice in another's opportunity to forgive. It calls for an honesty that no longer expects perfection from oneself, that pardons and shows mercy as God himself forgives and loves in the very forgiving.

Christian forgiveness, then demands a largeness of heart that is not without a strong element of realism. It is not to be mistaken for that unkindness which lets everything and anything go uncorrected. It is a forgiveness made real in that most neglected of community exercises, fraternal correction. In a lengthy passage in Matthew's gospel, the duty of brothers to correct each other is phrased in stern and undeniable terms. "If your brother does something wrong, go and have it out with him alone, between your two selves. If he listens to you, you have won back your brother. If he does not listen, report it to the community, and if he refuses to listen to the community, treat him like a pagan or a tax collector." (18:15–18) This is one of the least professed evangelical counsels. The directives seem clear enough; but the courage required to put them into effect remains far from most community members. How often the faults of a person are allowed to harden until they are almost so much his face and form that community realists announce, "It is hopeless to try to change him." How often a discordant note between friends is passed over "in charity" but not forgotten, so that eventually the whole harmony of this personal relationship becomes discordant. Faults that are publicly discussed and common knowledge in community often never receive the kindness of fraternal correction, until finally they must be handled with the stern justice of an authority figure.

To correct a brother is kindness; it is to be a real brother to him. It is to love another enough to permit a temporary hurt for the sake of greater healing and health. It is to help a brother-being-redeemed. But it is also to take a risk, for the one corrected may respond in anger. Consequently, only a brother can risk correcting another. For it is only someone who truly loves, who will support the initial pain, risk the other's countercharges, bear the burden of listening to the other in his suffering. Only a brother can correct another, not in anger and as an expression of his own hurt but for the sake of the other. Only someone who is really formed in community will be capable of such an enduring love that the brother who has been corrected will know, must know, that the pain is love and therefore is redemptive.

Practically speaking, such fraternal correction can be a great strength in the formation of true community. Instead of the dishonesty that pretends to ignore another's faults, that lets another go on hurting both himself and the community, there is the support of brothers helping each other to face their problems in honesty and so grow in freedom.

If only a community could be formed in such fraternity, then what possibilities for growth could it not offer its members. Any member who found that the actions of another, even when not wrong in themselves, were still a source of constant irritation, could say so. This would prevent the initial soreness from growing into a spreading source of infection and dissatisfaction. He could say to his brother, "You know, what gets me about you . . ." secure that his brother would be free enough to answer in love, "And what gets me about you. . . ." In this way, both could say, "I love and trust you so much that I risk your present irritation for the sake of our deeper relationship. I love you enough to accept your limitations and also to know that you want to avoid giving pain to any other of the community."

In more serious matters, greater honesty is called for. This is no longer just a problem to be settled between two brothers; it is a community problem, something from which many others suffer. A brother has "done something wrong" and so is hurting himself and hurting the community by depriving it of a brother's growth in love. To say that such serious problems do not exist in religious congregations is completely unrealistic. How tragic it is when a member of a community is only told the truth about himself after many years of polite evasions. How sad that a pastor must finally tell a teacher, "Your anger is hurting the children more than your teaching is helping them." How pitiful when a religious whose change has been requested by many superiors, because he has never really entered into community, only comes face to face with his problem after twenty years of religious life. What a loss, not only to the individual, but also to the community, which must honestly accept its share of blame for what is now an almost hopeless situation. If only the formative influence of a community that really believed in fraternal correction could have helped such members to face themselves long before, then the accent could have been on the fraternal and not on the corrective element. Healing and redemption could have been effected by the support of brothers who truly loved.

Such fraternal correction can be an excellent indicator of how well formed a community really is, since it provides concrete evidence of truth and freedom among its members. It can also be formative of such a supportive community because it is a most realistic expression of, "He is my brother."

Suffering as forming community

Suffering, in all its many human forms, is not only a built-in part of living in community, it is also a strong formative influence. The unifying power of suffering is a matter of everyday experience.

Shared suffering calls for a kind of participation that almost nothing else can duplicate, for it strips persons of their defenses, makes known their mutual need, and allows others to take part in their pain.

Perhaps an unidentified element of Stoicism in the tradition of some congregations has dictated that suffering should be borne in silence. But pain too great for words can still be shared; silence can be shared. Suffering need not be discussed, often should not be discussed in its more personal aspects. But it can still be admitted, and such admission that one is in need strengthens community by calling on the concern of all. Such shared suffering is much less likely to end in the bitterness of pain that is never accepted. For suffering that is hidden, sometimes even from the sufferer himself, can end up by closing a person off from community. Here, suffering does not unify, it divides. One who hides his pain cuts himself off from his brothers, and ultimately no one may be able to penetrate the protective barriers and call him back to community. Such suppressed suffering can even cause a person to protest any attempts of his brothers to support and help him. In this way it brings on a gradual corrosion of person and community relationships. Suppressed suffering can even close a person away from the truth that is himself. He becomes secretive and hostile. Fear and anxiety spread with all the uncontrolled growth of cancer cells and radical surgery may prove to be the only cure.

Sometimes, however, this bitterness expressed by an individual may come, not from his failure but from that of the community. A brother who is in pain may find that the community does not accept his particular kind of suffering. He may discover that physical pain, loss of relative or friend is met with sympathy and understanding. But the subtler and still more painful afflictions of temptation, doubts, darkness may be ignored or met only with ill-advised attempts at good cheer. The individual's need to have some solitude in his suffering may not find acceptance. He may not be allowed sufficient time to heal.

Only suffering accepted by individual and community together can bring redemption and healing. Each person needs community acceptance in order to remain open in his time of suffering; for the suffering that is most needed by the individual is also that which is most painful, so painful that it can hardly be recognized at first sight as having much to do with redemption and growth in love. This is when a brother most needs another to say, "You are being redeemed in and through this experience, and I love you in your pain."

Unaccepted suffering, at best, is wasted suffering. And certainly there is sufficient suffering today to make this need of acceptance ever more critical. If only the liberal could learn to be compassionate with the pain of the conservative who finds the values of his whole life threatened. If only the conservative could grow in understanding of the impatience of the liberal who dreams another dream and wants to live another way. The pain of those who are leaving community also needs understanding and accepting love, for most of those who leave community after many years admit to leaving a part of themselves behind. Certainly they leave the richness of years of service that calls for grateful acceptance.

Even the questioning of those who are struggling with problems of vocational commitment calls for shared suffering, and out of this shared struggle can come a deeper sense of loyalty for all. Those who decide to remain in community need the support of their brothers to make firm their purpose. Each person who remains in religious life today must suffer through the questions implied by those who criticize religious life, through the pain of coming to newer realization of what is still lacking in their own community. It is in and through times of such crisis that members of community can form renewed communities strong in the support of their mutual suffering.

Finally, the community divided on the meaning of renewal needs to suffer through this together if the issue of their conflict is ever to be fruitful for the church. Congregations split by sincere differences that are tearing at the very fabric of their being need to be reassured that out of their honest suffering comes new unity. Even where actual division of a congregation must be effected, still the suffering shared in love promises fruitful new beginnings.

In all these ways, suffering forms community, forms persons in community. Failures that are accepted and forgiven promise redemption and point toward a heaven where there will be perfect community.

9 / The asceticism of community

If anyone tries to die to himself in any other way than living by Christ in glory, he will merely succeed in establishing in himself the rule of the flesh.

FRANCIS DURWELL, *The Resurrection**

THE TERM *asceticism* has a way of bringing out the most negative reactions in religious trying to live, to survive, in the midst of today's crisis of change and insistent demand for renewal or dissolution. It is as though just living today were asceticism enough. Another reason for this contemporary negative attitude is the frank realization that past practices, once held in such high esteem, are no longer believable. At one time, these practices seemed to promise perfection or at least be reliable indicators of progress toward it; but all too frequently they failed to produce anything more vital than a pattern of behavior. And more often than most religious would wish to admit, even that pattern had elements which contemporary psychology would consider somewhat harmful to full human development.

In the face of such reasons for present day negative attitudes, there seems particular need for communities to re-form their thinking on asceticism, to see it in the light of contemporary emphasis on person and community, to renew and adapt their ascetical practices to the needs of today.

*(New York: Sheed and Ward, 1960), p. 348.

Meaning of Christian asceticism

Christian asceticism, first of all, is not a veiled contempt for the world, nor a desire to exercise moral control over man's natural faculties, nor even a remote preparation for mystical experience. The above are motivating forces behind the ascetical practices of the Stoics, the Greeks, and the Orientals. But they are in sharp contrast with Christian asceticism's focus on man's here and now participation in the death-resurrection of Jesus. "It is Christian asceticism when a man verifies that his preparedness for death is existentially serious and inwardly genuine by freely laying hold upon something of the passion of death above and beyond that which destiny imposes on him."[1]

Christian asceticism, then, is centered on life in Christ. This is its meaning. Christ came to his resurrection through death on the cross; the Christian comes to Christ through the asceticism of his own daily dying. As Paul has summarized it, "Always, wherever we may be, we carry with us in our body the death of Jesus, so that the life of Jesus, too, may always be seen in our body. Indeed, while we are still alive, we are consigned to our death every day, for the sake of Jesus, so that in our mortal flesh the life of Jesus, too, may be openly shown" (2 Cor 4:11–12). The key characteristic of Christian life is its paschal character. It is a dying, but only for the sake of fuller and more abundant life. Christian asceticism remains, then, a means; it can never be an end. Its whole meaning is found in terms of the new life that it makes possible. It is for the sake of love and opens the way to greater love.

Such is the positive meaning of Christian asceticism: it is dying daily in order to live and love. But it is a dying. To what must a Christian die? To himself, to his egocentrism that sees everything in a circle closed about himself and tightly guarded; to that self-absorption that makes him ceaselessly orbit about himself asking anxious questions such as: What is in it for me? How do I look in the mirror of this situation? What do these people think of me?

A man's first renunciation, then, is the giving up of illusions about himself. One of these illusions is the safety of an asceticism that helps to guarantee a self-styled pattern of holiness. Holiness is never an achievement of man; it is always a gift of God. Man's asceticism can only be an emptying of his hands, a relaxing of the grip of willfulness, so that God may form him and make him holy. It is almost a truism that God's gift of holiness to an individual is so different from his expectation that, at first glance, it may seem no holiness, no gift, at all. Only a man who is willing to put aside his self-design of holiness can reach out in acceptance of such a gift of God.

A second essential element in any renunciation is a very basic acceptance of self. Only the man who has begun to love himself—as God loves him—can begin to be a Christian ascetic. For only a man who accepts himself as one loved can dare to face what is unreal in himself. Only a man who is secure in faith, firm in the belief that he is loved by God, can risk going out of himself in humble and admitted need of others. The Christian ascetic, then, is one who loves himself enough to leave himself in the faith and the hope that such death-to-self is the beginning of new life in Christ Jesus.

The Christian's passage from death to life includes both self-renunciation and self-development.

> In order to be united, you must first of all be yourself as completely as possible. And so you develop yourself and take possession of the world in order to be. Once this has been accomplished, then is the time to think about renunciation; then is the time to accept diminishment for the sake of being in another.[3]

The vision of Teilhard summarizes in clear terms the two poles of asceticism; the one, a growth in all that is positive and good in the self; the other an acceptance, perhaps even a free seeking, of self-renunciation as another means to greater love. Both polarities of growth and death are integral to Christian asceticism. In fact, Teilhard goes on to speak of an "inseparable alliance between these two terms." At the same time, he points toward the "continual and then the final ascendency of the second over the first."[3]

Just as asceticism is basically paschal in its orientation, so too its practice is essentially incarnational. Asceticism to be both Christian and human must be embodied, expressed in the concrete here and now; it cannot be left to the spirit of renunciation and the desire of laying aside self-illusions. But as soon as asceticism is embodied, it is exposed to enormous risks. Most dangerous of all, asceticism can become so identified with its embodiments that what began as self-denial ends up as a self-satisfying achievement.

Practically speaking, this means that asceticism must be subjected to the constant test of real effectiveness. It must express a real change in one's life, a *conversion* in one's relations to a neighbor. As Bernard Häring has pointed out, "All ascetical practices which do not result in greater willingness to serve and more sensitive awareness of the needs of others are untrue to life, pass life by."[4]

A similar critique can be made of certain ascetical practices which remain just practices. Asceticism cannot be an extra practice for the Christian, something in which he indulges occasionally. It must be incorporated into his life. It is obvious that there is a numerical limit to the number of practices that anyone can undertake; in fact, the law of diminishing returns seems operative here. But there is no limit on attitude of mind that allows for ever greater openness to the Spirit—without counting the all too obvious cost to self.

For the Christian the question is not. How difficult is this? but rather, How relevant is this to my growth in love? In other words he asks, Does this act which here and now embodies my openness make me more myself? Does it free me to be myself, to relate in love to others? Or is it another bond, another prop for my self-respect? If life and love of others call for me to disregard this particular ascetical practice, do I find that I am free to respond or am I caught, weighed down, by a burden which I alone have decided to take up? Thus there emerges a general criterion of Christian asceticism: the freedom to live in love. Other criteria which also serve to distinguish true self-denial from its counterfeit are the tests of truth, unity, orientation toward others, surrender in peace and in joy.

Asceticism in community

In the preceding section, with its emphasis on life and love as the essential orientation of asceticism, there have already been suggested some of the communal aspects of this participation of the Christian in the death-resurrection of Jesus Christ. Asceticism is the renunciation of self-absorption, false dreams of self-designed holiness, along with the discipline necessary for true self-growth. The criterion of ascetical practices is greater freedom for love and service. All of which suggests that the meaning of true ascetical practice is closely bound up with formation in community.

For one thing, true asceticism must be based on a realistic regard for persons. Above all, it must respect the individual's freedom, since its whole goal is to free, to redeem. It must begin with the needs of this person, at this particular time in his life. It must go on to consider the needs of the community, its particular problems, responsibilities to the larger community of church and world. This in turn underlines the great need of the individual for honesty with himself and with others. Each man begins with his own need for conversion; he asks the question: "What must change in me to prepare a way for the Lord?" Here the members of a community stand in special need of each other. For who can say in perfect truth which areas of his life are most in need of change? Who can determine, by himself, the most effective means to realize this conversion? Out of honest community dialogue emerges a picture of what this individual most needs in order to share more fully in community and so grow in the life of Christ himself. Such a willingness to change those things about oneself which cause others to suffer can be a very realistic way to embody one's willingness to "be consigned to death every day" (Rom 8:36). It is also a beautiful and authentic witness to one's desire to form and be formed by community.

Acceptance of those sufferings which are part of just living closely with others, the rub of variant personalities, the challenge to generosity called for by pluralism of ideas and ideals—all these are part of allowing oneself to participate in community. As someone has somewhat facetiously suggested. "This is the new look in hair shirts and they come in many sizes. Trying to live cheerfully with a neighbor who is irksome, doing kindness to a less attractive associate, accepting with equanimity the routine of life, your own failures."[5]

Positively, asceticism in community needs to be related to the response, here and now, of a particular local community. Members of the community need to ask themselves: What more can I give? Am I responsible for my brother, loving enough to correct him, to permit him to correct me? Am I contributing to the creative vision of this community, taking part whole-heartedly in its task? Am I willing to change, to respond affirmatively to the needs of different individuals, at different times, in inconvenient circumstances, even when their requests are inopportune? In the succinct phrasing of the Rule of Taizé, "To carry the burden of others, accepting the petty injuries of each day so as to share concretely in the sufferings of Christ: This is our first discipline."[6]

In summary, is the asceticism of a particular local community leading to greater unity? For unity is always one of the signs of the authentic Christian. Ascetical practice should never divide a person from himself, in strain and unnecessary tension. It should not separate him from his work, his friends, those he is called to serve. On the contrary, asceticism should have as its goal the gradual elimination of whatever may prevent unity in a person, in a person community. Any self-doubt that nibbles away at a man's dedication, any fear that leaves a man unfree, any holding back of one's talents that stems from immature and self-centered humility: all of these introduce elements of disharmony and strain in an individual's response, and ultimately will lead to some discord in community. In a comparable way, anything that closes a community in on itself, that prevents its members from being available to each other and to the wider community calls for some dying. In the strong words of Bernard Häring, "Whatever makes it difficult for others to approach the church must go, whatever prevents unity must go."[7]

Communal asceticism, then, is basically apostolic. "Just as the Son of Man came not to be served, but to serve, and to give his life as ransom for many" (Mt 20:28) so too, the religious will see asceticism as essentially a going out to others in redemptive love. In this sense the creative task of community will demand asceticism of its members and also structure their ascetical practice and test its genuineness.

Contemporary ascetical practice

Given the preceding principles concerning the meaning of Christian asceticism, with particular emphasis on its communal aspects, what follows in terms of renewal of ascetical practices?

First of all, renewal and adaptation of these practices is not to be equated with their elimination. Granted that the asceticism of today's religious will no longer find the expression of former times particularly appropriate, still this is not to conclude that no such practices are needed now. It is rather to suggest that asceticism for today must be related to life today. Since constant change is so much a part of contemporary culture, it follows that ascetical practices will be subject to the same kind of wide and constant variations.

In contrast to the past, when particular forms of discipline were made part of a man's "way of life," today it seems more appropriate that the only constant should be constant openness. In short, contemporary asceticism can never be programmed into the life of an individual, nor into the practices of a renewing community. Nor can a safe *standard* be suggested, considering the differing needs of individual persons and particular communities. Too little asceticism will be harmful, too much may be equally damaging. It has been wisely pointed out that, "In the spiritual life, as in all organic processes, everyone has their optimum and it is just as harmful to be beyond as not to attain it."[8]

Flexibility and responsibility seem the most appropriate forms of contemporary ascetical practice. Flexibility will demand of a man a kind of self-giving that can never be *achieved,* and so can never be made into a subtle form of self-satisfaction. It will keep a man open to changing needs, both in himself and in others. It will make him sensitive and so increase his capacity for loving and for suffering. Responsibility will prevent flexibility from degenerating into whimsy and unthinking going along with whatever occurs. Response evokes in man a demanding honesty, the simplicity and freedom to answer as he is; the daring trust in others which allows him to appear as he is, without protective mask and layers of acceptable camouflage.

Responsibility will also demand that members of community respond to each other and to their mutual task. This will again prevent an asceticism, no longer safeguarded by the definiteness of a program, from degenerating into no asceticism at all. To respond to the needs of a brother requires a constant and insistent self-giving. It also demands a giving up and a giving in to others that has always characterized true asceticism.

The beauty of such flexibility and response at the heart of communal asceticism is the realism of these practices. When community is really formed, the members who are forming it, being formed themselves in the process, find that asceticism is no longer just *a* practice in their life; it is an integral part of their way of living. There is no need to design ways of dying to self. Today's living-with-others ensures such opportunities.

The very real demands of one's brothers also call for those forms of asceticism which are most needed by the individual and so are most painful, but also most promising of new life. Community demands silent listening and the discipline of laying aside one's own preoccupations to give to another. It also requires patience from the man who is always in a hurry, and decisiveness from the person who is inclined to put things off. The quiet man finds that he must respond in love to the exuberance of those who are more out-going. In doing so, he will die to what might be a selfish solitude. The lonely religious will be asked to rejoice with another's good fortune and so his own pain will not harden into self-pity and bitterness. The man whose outgoing good cheer is more a matter of heredity and health than any particular practice of virtue will learn something of his brother's darkness and so will grow in compassion.

In short, community asceticism will find some of its strongest practical applications in and through community with its built-in need for communication. As Eugene Kennedy has realistically pointed out, the community man must be

> prepared to face the consequences of being willing to communicate. He must be ready, in other words, to die to himself in order that his understanding may be fully alive. He dies to deafnesses that have previously filtered out what others have tried to say. He dies to the fatigue that would have him put others off. He must be ready to die to the distractions which may flood his mind and carry him out of the present conversation. He must, in a word, come to life as person himself, if he is to be a person who even begins to understand.[9]

All of the above are realistic ways in which life in community calls for dying but also calls forth new life in its members. Part of this new life will be the response which the members give in developing and sharing their talents. To develop one's gifts calls for the humility of gratitude, as well as the realism of hard work. Not merely to develop one's talents but at the same time to put them at the disposal of others is to expose oneself to almost constant opportunities for giving self away. The scholar and the teacher, the carpenter who keeps the mission buildings together, the cook who makes meals into feasts, and the administrator who is on the firing line of demand and criticism—all will find that their very gifts are signs of the cross.

Another aspect of giving away oneself with one's gifts is the free acceptance of the gifts and the giving of others. Sometimes it may mean the help of a brother, when one would prefer to work alone; at another time it may mean receiving as a gift what one does not need. But to receive is to be grateful; it is to express that interdependence and responsibility that are basic to forming community.

Turning from community within to community without, it has already been suggested that asceticism today is an integral part of a community's response to its task in the world. A few practical suggestions might be made about how task shapes and structures a community's ascetical practices.

For one thing, the asceticism of today's apostolate will be formed in response to a pluralistic world. A man's desire to serve many, widely different persons will call for the asceticism of constant search for new ways of communicating, more appropriate language, newer, better ways of serving. So the apostle will find such constant calls on his adaptibility one of his most real ways to deny any tendency to self-complacency. In a world where the generation gap seems ever wider, where persons who are less than a decade apart chronologically find that they can no longer understand each other, no man can settle down into a patterned response. In a church where the confusion of means with ends, that results from excessive legislation, calls for new efforts on the part of every Christian to live as a Christian, the religious will find that he must die to the security of having answers. In a world where there is increasing conflict between the "haves" and the "have nots," the religious man can seek to discover an asceticism based, not on renunciation, but on "the appropriate and reasonable use of goods and means, which in the circumstances means a harder discipline than a plain renunciation."[10]

In all these forms of renewed ascetical practice the individual religious, as well as the community, will find himself meeting one of the most difficult demands of today: the constant risk, sometimes the realization, of failure. Widely differing needs, rapid change, the challenge of the generation gap—all have built-in possibilities of failure, but a failure that can be redeeming. For all demand the asceticism of beginning over and over again, the discipline of admitting mistakes, the dying to self that says from the bottom of one's heart, "I can go no farther; God help us all."

Today, the needs of the world are so multiple, the problems so complex, that no person, no community, can even begin to "do it all." This is where Harvey Cox suggests that "today's asceticism" calls for a "focusing of energy on what is important at the cost of denying what is less important."[11] This results in a frank admission of limitations (surely a form of dying), accompanied by a realistic effort to determine what can be done here and now (which is to opt for life and to live it fully).

Deciding what can be done here and now demands community dialogue, and such communication can be a meaningful asceticism of today's apostolate. For a group to determine its task, to decide what are the best ways of accomplishing it calls for much give and take. In fact, the detachment demanded by such re-appraisal, the giving and receiving of talents and gifts, the fraternal correction that might be needed—all of these are particularly appropriate forms of communal penance. For, a community is not just a group of individuals who, individually, are to practice asceticism. They are to live together in community and to die together in community. They are mutually responsible for their living and their dying, as together, the community is being formed by its shared participation in the death-resurrection of Jesus.

10 / Temptations against community

evil may not be seeing well enough
so perhaps to become less evil we need only to see more
see what we didn't see before and here everybody is in the game
things look different to different people depending on where they stand
and if we can only share views, not convert others to our views
we would get a larger vision
no single group can do it alone   the job is too big
and we can only make it
if we work it out together.

SISTER CORITA, *Footnotes and Headlines**

MAN IS already redeemed; he is already free; heaven is open; heaven is now. Alleluia! But man is also still-being-redeemed; he is becoming free, working out his salvation in the here and now of very real struggle, dying to self in order to come to new life in Christ Jesus.

In the previous chapter the emphasis was on yet-to-be-redeemed man's need for asceticism, both individual and communal. This chapter will focus on those elements which threaten to destroy community and which must be resisted, if community is ever to be formed. These elements can, in the very crisis they occasion, call for a new decision to enter community, to open oneself to forming and being formed by community.

It has been suggested that man's original sin was a failure in community, a failure in true self-understanding, as well as a failure in collaborating with God and with fellowmen. Man began to play a role and so could no longer truly communicate with God or with himself. The most immediate practical consequence was man's diminishment of himself and his fellow men. Unity and community were fragmented by this original crack in man's personhood, in his

*(New York: Herder and Herder, 1968), p. 26.

relationships with other persons, with God, and this has been the original source of all the disunion and failures in community that have followed man down the ages. Wars, racial conflicts, ethnic struggles are obvious examples of fragmented community. Political divisions in the church, reform parties, and schisms are comparable evidence that the Body of Christ is still lacking in full growth and maturity. Divorce, separations, and family quarrels that harden into feuds make the same original crack apparent in the life community of the family.

So it is only realistic to expect that religious communities will also be fragmented by party politics, by sharp and sometimes real divisions, with consequent breakdowns in communication that harden into bitterness and defeatism. Every congregation knows something of these original sins. Fortunately, such failures in community have the dubious advantage of being very obvious. What are less apparent and so, more dangerous, are those temptations against community which threaten its realization but do not immediately appear as destructive. They are the small illnesses that sap vitality, the cracks in the sidewalk that cause a man to stumble, the falling plaster that is indicative of sagging corners or a leaking roof.

Temptations against community have the psychological advantage of most temptations. At first, they seem insignificant, a little giving in to self, some yielding to discouragement, an expression of jealousy, a selfishness that expects too much of others. In themselves these are small things but they can eventually eat the heart out of persons in community. In a similar way a community may turn in on itself, making itself the purpose of its being, in a kind of selfish isolationism, sacrificing individuals "for the sake of the greater good." These are all temptations of a community that eventually destroy its credibility because they destroy its unity.

Temptations of persons against community

Living in religious community does not carry a built-in guarantee of fewer temptations. It seems truer to say that the temptations of the religious man will be more directly related to religion, as indeed might be expected. A sensual man will find his trials, his triumphs, his failures, in the very sensuousness of his nature. In a comparable way, the religious man will be tested in terms of his religious character. He will be tried in such a way as to reveal what manner of man he is, whether he is truly religious or only pseudo-pious. Similarly, a man called to live in person community can expect that his temptations, his testing will be in the area of his living with others, his acceptance of his mutual responsibility and solidarity of salvation.

Reinhold Niebuhr has pointed out that "The chief source of man's inhumanity to man seems to be the tribal limits of his sense of obligation to other men."[1] He goes on to explain that "Any distinguishing mark between the 'we group,' in which mutual responsibilities are acknowledged and a 'they group' which are outside the pale of humanity may serve the tribal character of humanity."[2] The reference to man's tribal character seems to put him back on the level of the primitive, but the division of the "we" from the "they" is all too easily recognizable as a carry-over from man's original lack of unity. Someone has suggested that the use of "they" and "them" could be good indicators of how far a group has progressed toward community.

The basis for such primitive fragmentation is clearly described by Niebuhr "in terms of man's limited sense of obligation to other men;" in short, his sense of "ir-responsibility." This, it seems, is every man's temptation against community; his failure to respond. This original temptation takes many forms, ranging from isolation to over-identification, from tendencies to objectify community, to "techniques of degradation."

One of the most real temptations for man in community is his tendency to jealousy. To respond to the gifts of others without constantly making comparisons with one's own gifts and to express appreciation for others' contributions, without expecting, much less demanding, equal appreciation for oneself are tests of true community spirit and call for the asceticism of self-forgetfulness.

It has been suggested that jealousy is particularly a temptation within celibate communities. The reason given is the fact that the celibate does not experience the warmth and personal appreciation that should be part of a family's being-together. The celibate has no wife to give him the support of her daily concern; no children to whom "father" and "mother" are extremely important persons, the "wisest" and the "best," at least in the young child's eyes. It is also true that the celibate in religious community does not experience those external measures of success and personal achievement given by promotions, increased salary, ability to own more and better quality objects. Lacking the personal appreciation of a family and the more impersonal evaluation of job status, the religious may tend to seek overcompensation from community. To some extent the religious has a positive right to support from his fellow celibates, to receive encouragement and evaluation of his contributions. These are positive human needs and must be met. But on the other hand, to expect a religious community to provide a "family" is to expect it to be what it is not. For a religious community is never a life community of persons united by natural ties of family, race, ethnic background. Nor is it purely a society with emphasis on getting the job done.

Over-concentration on one's need for appreciation can take the form of jealousy, since the achievements of others in community then become a threat to oneself. Because community is formed through mutual responsibility, the focus of the individual must be "out," on others, seeing and appreciating their gifts, responding to their needs. Appreciation of one's own gifts and talents is a consequence of true community, not its goal.

Focusing too much on having one's own needs filled by community is a self-defeating process, since it is destructive of both community and person. A sensitivity to the needs of others and the capacity to respond form community. Failure to go out to others gradually destroys the community by destroying the relationship of persons in community. Ultimately such a concentration on self will leave the self more isolated and unappreciated than ever. And this is the road to bitterness.

Another basic need, which may become a temptation in the name of community, is a failure to respect another's need for solitude and privacy. Anything that threatens a person's privacy is a violation of community. Such temptations are particularly dangerous in a group whose desire to build community still has something of the over eagerness of the adolescent. In an attempt to "be open," to "communicate on the level of personal experience," there may be some danger of violating another's right to privacy. For community and privacy are not opposed, since privacy is part of being a human person and community can only be formed in terms of persons, and the gradual humanizing of their being. Forced self-revelation, pressure brought to bear on another's inability to "open-up" at a particular time or place, failure to respect the individual's need for solitude— all of these are temptations against true community.

On the other hand, persons in community must constantly be on guard against their own tendencies to isolate themselves from community as a whole or from certain members of community. Privacy is a man's right to certain aspects of himself where another may come only by invitation. But this is quite different from an isolationism that simply withdraws more and more from community, that fails to respond to others in community. Perhaps the latter point is the key difference, distinguishing solitude from selfish withdrawal. Does a person seek to be alone for the sake of a fuller being with others? Is his desire for privacy accompanied by deepening respect for others?

In contrast, isolationism is withdrawal for the sake of oneself. It is a preoccupation with self that does not permit being present to others; it is a turning in on self that makes the focus of one's life no longer "we" or even "they" but "me." Anything that causes "me" to be spelled in capital letters threatens to diminish community.

Such compensations as jealousy and isolationism will eventually result in a kind of apathy that simply gives up on community. As has been suggested, forming community, allowing oneself to be formed in community, is one of those *everyday* affairs. Temptations to apathy manifest themselves as failure to enter community every day, refusal to be always beginning over again. Holding grudges, going back to "he said," reviewing past mistakes, failing to forgive sincerely are all tendencies that test a man's willingness to keep faith in community, to accept the "day to dayness" of living with others. Once faith in others in community has been lost, the result is a kind of apathy and a giving-up that damages the spirit and vitality of a group.

One reason for apathy is the failure to find in community what one has expected to discover there. Every person enters community with certain dreams of his own. This is natural and also part of the vision he contributes to forming the community. What is damaging is the temptation to despair when one's expectations are not met. Someone has very aptly described the symptoms of such disillusionment in the life of a Sister:

> She never thought that life in the convent would be as it is . . . She finds so many faults among the Sisters . . . She looked for a life given over to nobility of action, and so much pettiness exists. She never expected Sisters to be so capable of fault-finding, of misjudging, of being haughty, of being lazy, or of being so vain, so picayunish.[3]

Every man could add to this list his own shattered dreams and his personal disillusionment. But such adding to a list would prove very little about community, except for underlining the obvious fact that community is human. What it might prove would be something about an individual's capacity to overcome temptations to discouragement.

Once again, this tendency to expect perfection and be unreasonably disappointed when one's expectations are not met seems one of the particular hazards of the religious man. The capacity to leave one's dreams, to be open to the unheard of possibilities of God's desires is some sign of an individual's capacity to be formed in the community of the people of God. This almost universal temptation to escape from the more discouraging aspects of reality into one's privately designed dream world is part of what community is meant to *test*. For community is no man's dream; it is God's promise; it is built on the faith of brothers. So any man who truly wants to form community must resist, with the help of the other members of community, any temptation to substitute his plans, his dreams, for what God is making real through this particular local group.

Temptations to discouragement, it seems, can best be met by honest confession, calling forth the encouragement of one's brothers. A disillusionment that is once disclosed has had its sting removed. It can be healed, not by denial, but by facing the difficulty and by communal acceptance, in hope, of a community-yet-to-come. Such honest sharing of one's temptations to discouragement can also help an individual, aided by his brothers, to discover his personal responsibility for what is still lacking in the community. This counters any temptation to objectify community, to stand outside of it and to ask, "What's wrong with this community?" instead of asking, "What is wrong with *our* community?" "What is my responsibility for this?" "What is lacking in me?" For whatever is lacking in community is somehow a failure on the part of all its members. A congregation seeking to renew itself needs to remind itself that every member has helped to form the existing community. Each member can be part of what the community will become, if together all really want to risk forming community.

Another temptation against community, related to the former tendency to objectification, is a certain mistrust of community. Perhaps this is more realistically stated as a mistrust of authority in community, of a communal structure that has tendencies toward bureaucracy, of past failures to respond to the needs of individuals as individuals. In short, present mistrust may be based on very real reasons stemming from past fears. But no matter how real the reasons for past hurt, present mistrust can only be destructive of individuals in community and ultimately of community itself. Without trust, a person cannot respond, as he is; he can only live in hope of what the community can become. A temptation to mistrust based on past experiences, real or exaggerated, calls for the sympathy and understanding of other members of community. Mistrust can only be overcome by trust. The individual, on his part, must make what can be almost heroic efforts to risk entrusting himself once again to the community.

For one who has lost trust the only alternatives are either to leave the community, or, and this is the greatest temptation, to stay and yet remain outside of it in bitterness and cynical criticism. Every religious, at times, will find that his privacy has been violated, his need for encouragement neglected, his response rejected. At times the community in which he lives will seem shabby and worn. He will feel that his trust has been betrayed; his loneliness and disillusionment will begin to harden into cynicism and express themselves in hidden forms of anger. His temptation will be to destroy what has hurt him so much.

Gabriel Marcel once described with blunt realism those "techniques of degradation" which "poison the wells of human relationships." He climaxed his list with "suspicion, tale-bearing, physical and moral filth," explaining that these techniques were used by inmates in concentration camps to destroy each other in hope of some small personal gain.

Perhaps these "techniques of degradation" are too strong to be mentioned here. But they may suggest other techniques sometimes used in community: the anonymous note, the nasty criticism, the whispered gossip, the "Have you heard" and "I don't believe it" that certainly poison the wells of community. Hopefully such techniques of degradation will always be the exception. When and if they do exist, they destroy, first of all, the person who practices them. They dehumanize him; they make the trusting response of others almost impossible. Eventually they destroy community, leaving only the skeleton of structure, since the real life of the members must necessarily be lived elsewhere.

Temptations of communities

Since communities are not only the sum total of the individuals who compose them but are the "more" of true participation where the interaction of these individuals gives rise to a new reality, the corporate person of community, it follows that communities have their own identity, their own strengths, their own weaknesses, and consequently their own particular temptations.

Perhaps one of the greatest temptations of communities—the life community, the society, and even the person community—is the temptation to subordinate individuals to the group. That there will always be some tension between person and community has been a recurrent theme of this book. But out of such tension can come the creative reality of new forms. So the tension in itself is healthy. What is dangerous is any overemphasis on either one or other aspect. Individualism and collectivity are equally destructive of true community.

Persons can be subordinated to structure; the needs of the individual swallowed up by the demands of the institution. As a consequence, persons are diminished so that they will *fit* into the local group, so that jobs will get done, so that the community's external appearance will not be open to question. Creative individuals are either not accepted into the community, or, at least, find that they cannot be themselves and remain in community. Those whose talents are less productive of immediate results feel unwanted. Anyone whose present being-himself involves working through certain problems and difficulties, experiences the added pain of feeling that he is a burden to the community. In short, one of the temptations of community, threatening its very breakdown as community, is the tendency to *use* people in some way. "Man is precious capital" said Karl Marx, and he was right, in a sense. But man is so precious that he is beyond value, and hence can never be identified with any one measure of worth.

To use a man is to attempt to possess him and insofar as a man is able to be possessed, he is no longer a man. Just as parents must resist the temptation to *use* their children to fulfill their own ambitions, to compensate for their personal failures, so too, community must reject any tendency to use persons even "for the service of the church." Sometimes the very word *formation* can cover a subtle desire to shape persons in some kind of community image and likeness so that they will be more *useful*. But such molding of persons would destroy that pluralism which is one of community's greatest delights, its true *capital*.

Here community responsibility must take on a new dimension. No man can be forced. He cannot be made to conform, forced to live beyond his means. This is an area where community must be particularly on its guard. Persons develop differently and at different times; some more slowly, some more rapidly. What is prayer for one, could be only pretense for another. What is honesty for one, could be forced confession for another. Community can only respond, it can never demand. To compel a person to give more than he can afford is to risk his eventual bankruptcy as a person.

Perhaps some of the contemporary problems in religious life come from a kind of community oversell. Individuals, especially those *in formation,* have sometimes been forced to live beyond their personal means and such overextension can only lead to eventual breakdown. This means that communities must learn something of the patience of God who knows how to wait for man, to seek him out, but also to let him go; to welcome back a prodigal, but also to divide up the inheritance.

Present renewal, with all its consequent questioning, makes special demands on the patience of communities. Certain individuals who are just beginning to learn what manner of men they are must be given the opportunity to discover this for themselves. The results may be awkwardly adolescent. But only a selfish parent will deny his growing sons and daughters the chance to make some of their own mistakes. This is painful, especially for the parent, and religious congregations will find it difficult to watch adults go back and relive the experience they somehow missed along the way, and now make the mistakes that should have been part of their earlier maturation. But such is the reality of some present-day religious congregations which have to go from late nineteenth century to late twentieth century in a matter of a summer's chapter session.

Since the analogy of community to parent has been used in the above paragraphs, it seems necessary here to reject any temptation to form community according to the parental model. The members of a person community are and must be if they are to accept the mutual responsibilities of true community. Communities, therefore, must resist any temptation to act in a maternal or paternal fashion. What is being suggested above is that communities will experience some of the same temptations that test true parenthood: the tendency to use persons, to overprotect them, to demand more of them than they can give.

A person community of docile children is a contradiction in terms. A community that attempts to compare member with member in the false assumption that all should somehow be alike and therefore comparable, is equally contradictory. The Spirit, working in the church, in the religious congregation, is the Spirit of both unity and diversity. He gives different gifts and sometimes these, like the gift of tongues, create surface confusion. But all this is for the sake of greater eventual unity.

This brings us to another temptation of contemporary communities: their reluctance to take risks. So many persons are involved; so much hard labor of the past could be lost; individuals can get hurt. These are all good reasons for what may be a prudent decision not to undertake a new work, not to begin a certain experiment. But these can also be excuses that are more related to the reluctance of the bureaucrat than to the on-going development of leadership in a pilgrim church. To go on a pilgrimage always involves the risk of leaving home. So risk in itself cannot be sufficient reason for failing to consider the new and as yet untried. A vital community will have to take risks; the only alternative is to die. To live in community is always to be exposed to some danger. But it is to be alive.

One final temptation that seems particularly relevant to a period in history where community is so much talked about, so much desired, is the tendency for communities to turn in on themselves. As religious congregations, following the directives of Vatican II, take long, hard looks at themselves, they discover, all of them, that they are to some extent in need of renewal and reformation.

They are all a little ill, or let us say they are suffering. One of the temptations of anyone in pain is to become centered on his own problem, but this is only to increase the suffering. Just as a person going through an identity crisis needs, most of all, to forget himself in order to find himself, so communities suffering through renewal, with all the attendant pain and crisis of identity, need above all to forget themselves, to recall that their whole reason for being is "for others." Too much concentration on changing structures, on new formation programs, on new designs for line and staff functions in government can make a community nearsighted. Members of renewing communities need to keep in perspective the immediate problems of their city, the local parish, the almost insupportable burdens of the world community.

The balance of these outgoing concerns will not automatically happen. It will require the insight of each and every member to keep the community open and opening out. Study of world problems needs as much emphasis as the serious reading of the new theology. Practical concern with the problems of suburbs or inner city must be as much part of renewal programs as the development of greater understanding of collegiality and subsidiarity.

Granted that communities can be tempted to use their members, to subordinate them to structure, to reject pluralism and refuse to take risks, still these very temptations can become occasions for communities to reaffirm their true nature. Where a community respects persons and gives them priority over structure, where it trusts individuals enough to allow them to make their own mistakes, there the community turns away from self-centeredness and opens itself to the wider world. Every time a community, out of respect for its past, risks moving into the future, the Spirit is at work renewing the face of the earth.

11 / A community of believers

Faith, both presupposes the community and creates it; the courage to believe is born of a pentecostal event where many are gathered together in unity of purpose. Faith is our confidence in the personal experience of others.

K. RAHNER, *Belief Today**

WHAT DOES it mean to believe? What is implied in the phrase, *community of believers?* What is this inter-relationship of faith and community about which we hear so much today?

The relationship of love and community is apparent in theory, at least. For love is always the ultimate dynamic force moving the Christian community toward the glory of the resurrection. But love implies faith and hope. So here and now, faith and hope also form communities and keep them faithful to the promise of Christ that someday all will be one in perfect communion with the Father, with Jesus and the Spirit, with each other.

The inter-relationship of faith and community is a matter of constant theoretical reaffirmation: I believe in the holy, Catholic church. I believe in the community of saints. This relationship is also a matter of daily experience: To believe, one must be in communication with oneself, with another. So faith presupposes community, the possibility of coming to communion. Community, in its turn, purifies and tests faith. For it is with others and in

*(New York: Sheed and Ward, 1967), p. 56.

terms of others that the Christian asks questions about his faith and then tests the realism of his answers against the reality of Christian community, God at work in our times and our circumstances. Faith, then, creates community. Community also matures and strengthens faith. This dynamic interplay of faith and community, each forming the other, each formed by the other, is at the heart of true Christian belief.

Faith presupposes community

No one believes alone; we believe only in and through others. To believe is to enter into community, the community of those who trust and are trusting. So faith itself, presupposes the possibility, even some degree of actualization, of community. This same interrelationship of faith and community carries over to the content of faith and to the very possibility of being faithful.

This communality of faith is not just a matter of accidental association but follows from a true understanding of what it means to believe. For faith is personal, better still, it is inter-personal. Faith is a matter of *who* more than of *what,* since faith as object, the what I believe, is only affirmed in terms of the total person who is accepted. Faith does not focus primarily on assenting to the truth of what someone says, but rather on accepting the one who is speaking. Or to put it in other words, what one accepts is the truth that is this person, the message that is his word. What a person says is *true* when it is expressive of himself, his thought. So truth is always relational because it is always personal and a part of an individual's capacity for entering into personal relationships.

In *Creative Fidelity,* Gabriel Marcel describes faith as "giving or opening a credit account for someone."[1] To give another credit, especially to give him the unlimited credit of total credibility, is to trust him completely. It is, at the same time, to look beyond one's own resources, to open oneself totally to the needs and requests of another. So faith looks out on the other. But it also looks in to oneself as known, in relationship with others.

For it is only in relationship with another, that any one would dare to offer such total credit. Any attempt to reckon one's own resources, carefully to count one's store and so guard against any personal bankruptcy would be doomed to defeat. Who could extend total credit in view of his own limitations, his own poverty? And who could know and so evaluate his own or other's need that he could afford to offer such total access? Only mutual belief and trust make absolute credit possible.

Faith, then, is built on belief in another and on belief in oneself. These two aspects of faith are so inter-related that to deny one is to deny the other. And to ask which one comes first is to ask a chicken-egg sort of question that leads to endless circular, self-defeating reasoning. All of which indicates again that faith is always a matter of relating a "me" and a "thee."

But since beginnings must be made, and since faith in oneself is perhaps the more neglected pole, let us start with this. Perhaps the greatest act of faith a man makes is an affirmation of his own credibility. Any honest man can give a thousand reasons why he should never be given total credit. He knows himself so well and consequently faith is so difficult that false claims often replace true belief. To claim is to assert something; to believe is to assent to someone.

The basis of true self-acceptance is not a matter of "claim to fame" but of assenting to "that particle of creation which is me."[2] It is a certain willingness to accept the gift that is myself and to accept this as a gift. It is an acceptance of the fundamental human need to go beyond the objective evaluation of "I have certain gifts," beyond the even more radical affirmation of "I am gifted," and finally to come to the incredible realization of "I am gift." From this acceptance of oneself as gift flows the ability to give oneself. But this is not to suggest that first one must accept oneself and then, secondly, give oneself. For the dynamics of faith in self and faith in another are such that it is only in giving that one comes to see oneself as gift.

Such acceptance of oneself is also a constant, on-going process. Firm faith is not faith hardened in a certain stance, but rather a matter of ever-present fidelity. Since self can never be possessed, self-acceptance must be an "attitude of constant inner revision."[3] Such constant conversion is growth occasioned by ever changing relationship of self to another. It is response to the call of another, which call is reiterated in all the changing aspects of personal relationship.

All of this brings us back to belief in the other. Here faith is total acceptance of the other as he is in himself; it is also an appeal to the person he can become. Such an appeal is likewise a critical factor in his becoming. Who has not experienced the potentiality of having someone say, "I believe in you. I know you can." Or who has not felt the destruction sown by another's unbelief.

Such fidelity, however, can never be demanded of another or of oneself. It must be free, if it is to be freeing. It cannot remain at the contractual level of pledged constancy and calculated risk. This is not to say that faith is to be identified immediately with uncalculated risk or presumption. Presumption is unwarranted just because it fails to take into account all the reality of risk, while faith simply looks beyond the reality of itself, its own resources. True fidelity is not based on what the other can become, what my own powers are, but rather on what we can become together. True faith, then, blends into hope and expectation of what is to come.

Fidelity to the other is never a simple, easy matter. Total trust comes hard, just as real self-acceptance must be paid for in the coin of self-renunciation. What must be given up is that tendency to specify and to limit that would attempt to keep faith under our own control and so deny true fidelity.

Faith, then, is another very profound example of that active receptivity which underlies so much of the Christian life. In the past, we have phrased this as: faith is a gift, an expression that hints at a materialist orientation to faith and gives rise to such problems as "Why do some receive this gift and not others? Perhaps it would be better to say that faith is a readiness to receive gifts. For all receptivity requires faith. Only a believer accepts a gift as gift, accepts another as one so loved that even his smallest offering is a present. Only the faithful man lives in enough loving expectation to untie the knots and begin to unwrap the package, believing fully that what lies hidden within is worth discovering.

Faith, then, is related to promises and opens to the future. A promise is a pledge of a self that is yet-to-be; it is a looking ahead in hope. In this sense Abraham is called the father of all the faithful, since he believed enough to accept God's impossible promise. Consequently, Abraham who was too old to father a child fathered a people, a community of believers. What was, humanly speaking, hopeless, became filled with hope and expectation for all generations to come.

Acceptance of gifts, of promises, obviously contains a strong element of passivity. The faithful man must also, to some extent, be the quiet man, even the silent man, so that he can hear another speak and can be open enough to receive truly his revelation. Part of this acceptance is also an activity keeping one always open to risk. Fidelity will be given not to beliefs but to the one who calls. True fidelity is silent, but it also speaks honestly and strongly. It is in this sense that belief flows into the active passivity of true prayer. To pray is to believe in community enough to communicate, to hope enough to look forward to communion.

Community tests faith

To believe is to enter into community, to accept the possibility of community, to be faithful in communicating with oneself and with another. This is the personal and the inter-personal aspect of faith that makes it essentially communitarian. But the content of faith is also oriented to the personal and consequently to the inter-personal.

The question: "What do you believe?" can tend to make faith an object with a consequent loss of its personal element. On the other hand, not to raise the question of content is to risk faith in false gods. For every man must believe in something, just because he is a man and finds himself drawn into personal relationships with others. Even the denial of faith, "I do not believe" is itself a faith-act. It denies another credit, which is a kind of affirmation that giving credit is a possibility.

The worshipping of false gods is not just a problem for the old pagan or the modern primitive; it is an issue for every man of faith. "Belief which is not belief is bad; belief in a god who is not God is worse."[4] Just as protestations of belief in another can conceal a real lack of faith, so too professions of religious faith can be commitments to a domesticated god made in our own image and likeness.

Faith must be constantly purified; it must be tested. And what tests faith is honest reflection on both subject and object of faith. The believer needs to look at who he is; he also needs to re-examine the content of his faith. To do this honestly he needs the help of others. Reflection, then, like faith itself, presupposes community and man's ability to commune within himself and with others. Individualistic reflection can end up in unreality. To prevent such deception and worship of what-is-not, every man needs to test his belief against the sharp edge of community reflection. This will serve to strengthen real faith and to question what is unfounded. It will enable faith to remain both free and constant. The man who doubts will be encouraged, both in his doubting and in his resistance to doubt. He will feel the support of the community to question what he must question; he will be confirmed in what he should retain and in what he should reject. In this way community reflection will help each man to grow in true faith.

History and personal experience confirm the danger of a faith that clings tenaciously to beliefs that should now be discarded. It is in this sense that Quentin Lauer asks: "The theologians of the sixteenth century condemned Galileo, but refused to look through his telescope; in that case who had the greater faith, Galileo or the theologians?"[5] The balance between a faith so riddled with questions that it is no faith, and the faith that is free enough to examine itself critically seems rooted in communitarian reflection. For each man's faith helps to build the faith of others. Why do we believe as we do? One of the main reasons is because we have made the beliefs of others our own.

It follows that one of the greatest needs of a community of believers is just such a statement of belief from its members, a statement that will challenge both the speaker and the hearer. "I believe," and the response should indicate the heartfelt faith of each member. Furthermore, a man can only reveal these beliefs of his in a community. He cannot speak in this way to the unbeliever; even if he should try, what is heard generally remains on the level of expressed opinion, and so is open to debate, even ridicule. But within community each man is freed to be himself, to be with others and enter into a faith relationship with them. What he expresses in such a community is his own unique revelation saved from the danger of those heresies which Gilbert Keith Chesterton once aptly described as truths gone mad with loneliness.

The more deeply a man enters into community, the more fully does he share faith with others. Whereas the mob or the crowd only share the instinctive acceptance of emotional values, men who form a life community share belief in the same life values. Men who live in a society relationship with their fellow men must believe in the benefit of such contractual relationships. But men who live together in a personal community share the same basic faith in the responsiveness and lovableness of each other. Such a sharing in faith ultimately is based on an absolute Thou who gives credit to all other men, who first believes in man, before man is. It is God who makes men faithful, whose faith is creative of every believer and every belief. This is the most essential element of any

Christian faith: belief in God's unconditional love for men; and, even more incredible, belief in his love for *me*. "This is the mystery of saving love that no string of propositions will ever tie down."[6]

Consequent upon faith in a God-who-loves-man is belief in man's capacity to be saved. But, "We cannot affirm that life is saved unless we believe that we can become friends and together build true community."[7] Hence faith must be operative here and now in the immediate circumstances in which one finds oneself. It is a faith that is tested against the ever present human reasons for disbelieving in God, the pain and suffering, the injustice of this world, and, above all, the scandal of his coming to us in all our weakness and lack of fidelity.

Only against the reality of such faith in the possibility of community and of communion can faith really be tested and purified. For belief in a god who is so transcendent that he never becomes involved in our world is too easy; it is also unchristian. Faith in God incarnate, God among us, is true belief. "The activity of Christian faith is not directed toward the existence of an all-perfect God, but toward the psychological uncertainty and contradictions inherent in our own experience of the developing Kingdom of Heaven already here present in the human efforts of the family of man to achieve maturing personhood."[8]

here Faith creates community

Not only does faith presuppose a community of believers who are in communion with themselves and with each other, but it is also true that faith is creative of such a community. This is particularly true of the person community, of which the religious community is only one example. In the person community the members are bound together by their relationship to each other as persons, and such a relationship must center around truth and love.

To know the truth of another, we must first believe in him. Even the initial tentative approaches of one man to another presuppose faith; otherwise the first encounter will remain on the a-personal level of use or, worse still, of threat. If a first meeting is ever to deepen into knowledge of persons, then there must be at least some degree of personal acceptance that must gradually develop into the mutual understanding which makes possible personal communication.

What is true on the level of simple human experience is likewise true on the more profound level of man's entrance into the Christian community. A man first hears the word of God through acceptance of the preaching of others. He listens and responds, and his initial response allows for further revelation, more profound communication. But if the community into which a man is entering is to be considered fully Christian, then what must be accepted is God revealing himself in the Christian community. In short, a man's faith implies an acceptance of the incredible fact that this community, this church, is a communion of saints. And this despite appearances to the contrary. Such faith, such expectation, is part of this community coming to full stature as a community of God's holy people. When a man believes this, and to the degree that he believes it, he too becomes holy, as he puts himself into communication with the whole body of faithful who accept the revelation of the Father in Jesus. The believer's faith saves him, makes him a member of the community of saints.

Faith not only enables a man to enter community, but also forms the bond that unites the members of the community. When men no longer believe in each other, no longer accept community as possible, then community *is* no longer possible. For when faith is lost, community is lost. Again, what is true in terms of any human community is also true in terms of the Christian community. When two persons who had once entered into some kind of truly human relationship with each other gradually begin to lose faith, they also lose the ability to communicate with each other. Infrequent, purely surface communication makes shared faith impossible; it also lessens the possibility of community. What once bound persons together, now only emphasizes their distance. They have nothing to say to each other because they have no common ground of shared faith, sharing in faith. Similarly when a man begins to lose faith, he finds himself cut off from the Christian community. He no longer shares the concerns of his brothers; he stands apart and makes his judgments, which, like all judgments, are basically directed against himself. The unbeliever excommunicates himself.

Such is something of the negative aspect of loss of faith and consequent loss of community. The positive inter-relationship is equally true. To share faith is to enter ever more deeply into community. Men who share only a few beliefs can communicate only in this restricted area; in other areas they do not really speak the same language. In contrast, when persons share a whole life-search for God, they have a common bond that transcends surface differences. Such is the bond of celibate religious community, where the members pledge a whole life's search for ultimate values.

As has been pointed out, "It is the very 'unclarity' and 'unpredictability' of God which has made us a community searching together."[9] We believe in God; we believe that God so transcends any conceptualization of ours that we accept the need for searching together. And we find that such mutuality strengthens our very desire to search. The search, in its turn, deepens our relationship with each other, our level of communication. Now we have something important to say to each other; for what we say no longer concerns just the small world of our immediate person but the whole community of men. As Christians we not only share the discovery but also support each other in the search. Believing is always, to some extent, a lonely business. Each man must answer for his own faith. But out of this very loneliness comes man's need for true community. The believer feels very keenly his own unbelief and so desires to be made firm in the faith of his brothers. This supportive role between believer and community, between community and believer, is emphasized in Jesus' words to Peter, "I have prayed for you, Simon, that your faith may not fail and once you have recovered, you in your turn must strengthen your brothers" (Luke 22: 32). Out of his union with the saving Jesus, Peter found new faith for the sake of the Christian community.

Unless faith is shared, no true community is possible. For it is this communality of faith which underlies common understanding and gives rise to consensus in decisions.

> We need not agree on everything but if there is no agreement whatsoever, there will be no genuine community. Still the deepest levels of community are found on the level of common commitments on decisions. It is here that we find the loyalty that binds the state together, the faith in the destiny of man which sustains us in periods of darkness, the fidelity which constitutes friendship and love.[10]

Community matures faith

Since faith creates community, it follows that community must also be vitally related to the gradual maturation of the faith-life. First of all, community supports the believer in his periods of non-faith. As has been suggested, "All belief, by the very fact that it is belief, is partially unbelief."[11] This implies that the believer and the unbeliever are not categories of man but indicators of the struggle that goes on in each man. At times, faith seems most in evidence; at other times, doubt darkens and almost extinguishes any peace in faith. During these latter periods, it is the community of believers who must sustain the doubter, even sustain him in his doubt. For that doubt must be faced or it will erode any true faith and lead to infidelity.

Community not only sustains the believer in his periods of darkness, it also serves to reveal the beginnings of real loss of faith. What are some of these signs? Unwillingness to listen, lack of commitment to others, despair rising from unfulfilled expectation, selfishness which is the *original* sin. These are all present to some degree in all men who are still being redeemed, but when they begin to become the basis for a man's whole view of self and reality, then faith is being destroyed.

In community a man is helped to discern these spirits of darkness. For these tendencies, though easily enough identified in others, have a way of disguising themselves and eluding every man in his own case. For example, every man thinks that *he* listens, that *his* expectations are justified. Even his own all-pervading selfishness has a way of hiding out and even disguising itself as a good. It is one of the roles of honest community living to reveal these tendencies to a man against the realism of his living with others.

Unfaith, then, can be countered by positive acts of faith, not just affirmations of assent to certain propositions but repentance for underlying causes of disbelief. Faith can be reaffirmed by beginning again to listen to God in whatever way he is revealing himself, by searching once more for true commitment in one's life, by moving out from self to service of others. These are acts of faith; they are also builders of true community.

On the positive side, community builds faith by revealing the true face of God who is community in himself. Only in a community can man learn, in terms of his own experience, what it means to know and be known, to love and be loved. Without such experience a man is left with abstract concepts of a God who is dead to him. It is in and through community that God reveals to man something of his own love and concern and tenderness. It is in the love of parents for a helpless baby that we see something of the total unselfishness of God's love of us. It is in the freshness of new life that we come to know the living God and in the joy of deep friendship that we begin to experience the existential meaning of "I have not called you servants but friends" (John 15: 15). Hopefully, every man could add to this litany of positive human relationships his own experiences that have lead to great faith in the true God.

But human community is not all unselfishness and new life and friendship. It is also struggle and pain and sacrifice. We are still experiencing the passion, as well as the first dawn of the coming

Kingdom. So, human community also reveals man's need for God. "When men find the horizontal values of justice, equality and love may drift out of control without vertical anchoring in some absolute, then they are existentially prepared to appreciate what a phrase like the 'people of God' might mean."[12] Perhaps it is one of the special graces of our time to realize that all our experiences of human organization and power have not made us a people. We still find ourselves torn apart by nationalism, by racism, by private and public greed. We need God, a God who can make us a people, a community of his faithful.

Out of this need for God, this need to share, a community is brought together and formed in faith. In community faith is expressed and heard. Here we can concretely reveal our belief: that God loves *us;* that he is acting in our world, even in the face of suffering and even especially in those areas where suffering touches us most deeply. In community we can affirm for and with each other our belief that God is with us, in these people. We can make real for ourselves, for each other, that community is possible, that God is making us believers, his faithful people. Together we can give lived witness to the power of God, "See how they love one another." For love is at the heart of what the Christian believes so that true community speaks of God and man and how they are related. This is to speak of faith in the language of one who is faithful.

12 / Prayer shared in community

What life have you, if you have not life together
There is no life that is not in community,
And no community not lived in praise of God.
                    T. S. ELIOT, "Chorus," *The Rock**

TODAY, ALONG WITH much concern for adaptation of structures and much discussion of temporalities such as budgeting and experimentation in small group living, there is also, interestingly enough, new emphasis on prayer and renewed search for ways of praying that will be meaningful in the contemporary context.

It seems that this search for new and more meaningful forms of prayer must begin with the lived experience of contemporary men and women of prayer. We must ask these men and women how they pray? What forms have they found to be effective in developing and deepening their own prayer life, in directing others to discover prayer? Only after these new forms of prayer have been lived with and tested in terms of long range effectiveness for expressing and promoting the growth of the Christian community, can serious reflection attempt to formulate the new prayer structures and develop a contemporary spirituality based on this prayer experience.

If prayer is to grow out of the experience of contemporary man,

*(New York: Harcourt, Brace, 1934), p. 21.

then it follows that some of the new understandings of self, of God, and of man in relation to God will be the theoretical basis for new prayer forms. Today, man sees himself, first of all, as a person, as one who makes himself in response to his world, whose project and goal is freedom and whose freedom is discovered in his relationship with others. Contemporary man is conscious that he is an historical animal, a being whose meaning comes out of a past, a person who is constantly opening into a future, a being who makes promises.

In short, contemporary man sees himself in the context of a person in community. He also sees God in the same context, as personalizing activity, as entering into personal relationship with man, as communitarian in the Trinity. At least such is the Christian conception of God. But contemporary man also finds that his God is an absent God, a distant God, a God who is no longer needed to "take care of" the world. For modern man, a God who is present among the lilies of the field and in the sheepfolds cannot be where he, man, is. Today man must seek ways of finding God in urban settings, in the swiftness of modern travel, in the complexity of modern machines. This is the God who must somehow be related to the shattering of life in today's world, where human abundance still leaves millions hungry and destitute, where women and children are the first victims of war, where destruction too terrible to imagine lies within the power of decision by a few men. Such, in very sketchy outline, are some of the considerations of modern man's coming to prayer. Add to this the breakdown of many forms of the traditional in society and the very slow development of new forms, and you have the prayer crisis of modern religious man.

Since prayer is so personal, since it grows out of man's experience of himself and his relationships with other persons, it follows that a serious mistake can be made by approaching this topic as though prayer were a problem, rather than a mystery. As a consequence, the "how to pray" question takes on something of the character of a demand, specifically a demand for a clear formula for success. In contrast, the acceptance of prayer as mystery, allows a quiet, reverent approach that seeks to participate in the prayer experience and is content to lay aside some of man's innate desire for comprehension and control. Such an acceptance of prayer as mystery is closely related to a deepening realization of prayer as an experience of communion and community, rather than a matter primarily for personal effort and concentrated diligence. The present chapter will explore some of the inter-relationships of prayer and community, the meaning of shared prayer in community, and then conclude with some suggestions on this expression of prayer in community. Before beginning, however, it might be well to point out that any discussion of prayer and community will suffer from a certain unavoidable vagueness. For community prayer must grow out of the life and experience of a particular community. It must be the prayer of *this* community and so will be individual and therefore indescribable.

Inter-relationship of community and prayer

The relationship of prayer and community, like all other personal relationships, is reciprocal so that prayer presupposes community, promotes and also expresses it. But it is also true that community presupposes prayer, results from prayer and makes true prayer possible. That prayer and community are so closely related seems an obvious conclusion from the basic description of prayer as communion and communication with God. What seems to need more emphasis is the connection between prayer and human community.

To begin with, prayer presupposes honest and loving community, union, with God, of course, but also with the human community. This concept is gospel-old, enunciated, as it is, in the command of Jesus that if a man comes to the altar with his gift and there finds that his brother has anything against him, that he leave his gift and go first and be reconciled with his brother and then come and continue his worship. For the God that we praise in prayer is the God of love, the God who loves each man with the long love of friendship. To attempt to respond to this God and yet ignore one's neighbor is to worship a false God, who is neither Father, nor creator.

Thus one of the presuppositions, as well as one of the prices of prayer, is the honest attempt to "go and be reconciled," not only with those whom the individual has himself offended but also with those "who have anything against him." This would mean taking the initiative in the reconciliation process, being the first to ask pardon, even the first to raise the question of the "why" of the strained relationship. Perhaps it is the latter which is especially difficult because it means a kind of exposure to the unknown "whatever" of the brother's grievance. It means asking the question, "What's wrong?" without being able to calculate the cost of the neighbor's reply. But it is out of such honest reconciliation that a man comes to prayer, humble and simple enough to be himself, poor and in need of forgiveness.

Prayer not only presupposes community with one's brothers; it also promotes such brotherhood. For true love of each and every man, in the gift of his uniqueness and in the reality of all his differentness, is beyond human resolution. Such love is a gift of God. And prayer prepares for this gift. The man who humbly asks God to let him give himself away in love will have his prayer heard. He will be given opportunities to love, will find that his heart begins to overflow with a love that transcends the prejudice of his own personal attraction, that takes even his natural gift of love and purifies it of an almost inherent selfishness. So prayer makes community possible. Those who find either prayer or community impossible might profitably ask themselves whether or not their problem arises precisely because they have failed to see how closely interlocked these realities are.

To pray is also to express a kind of belief in community. Perhaps this can be seen more clearly by expressing the negative: If community is not possible, then prayer is not possible either. For the negation of community would also involve the negation of communication in truth and in love. So there would be no possibility of prayer.

In contrast, if community is affirmed as a possibility—"I believe in the communion of saints," then communication is affirmed and love is expressed. In this expression of its love, community itself takes on something of the form and shape of its prayer expression. It is in this sense that prayer can be said to form a community by expressing the deepest desires of the community. As has already been suggested in Chapter 7, a community's expression of itself both forms the community and also grows out of the community's being formed. Like any word that expresses an idea and also, by that very process gives the idea its own form and reality, prayer gives expression to a community's belief in its own possibility and also gives this expression certain characteristics of gratitude and receptivity which mark it as Christian.

Finally what is expressed is man's experience of himself in his relationship with others. Even the prayer of alienation, or darkness and aloneness expresses a longing for community and for the at-oneness of true communication. Other prayer experiences are more obviously connected with man's existential knowledge of true community and express his joy and peace in communion. In any case, prayer presupposes both such negative and such positive experiences of community. Prayer expresses belief in the communion of sinners, as well as in the communion of saints.

Unless a man brings to prayer these fundamental human experiences of shared responsibility and shared guilt for wrong, unless he already knows something of the uplift and joy of truly human communication, it would seem that his prayer could only be formalistic expression of duty-filled petitions. It follows that one of the best preparations for fruitful prayer is a reflection upon one's relation with one's neighbor.

Such reflection should help to reveal the God who is present among men; the God who can be served by every cup of cold water given to one's brother. It would make real the demands of such a God and also help men to realize the needs of their own community. Prayer then can be described, in its broadest sense, as any response of man to God-among-men. In this sense, prayer is a means to community. In the strong terminology of Campbell and McMahon, "As a Christian community, we live the prayerful and united response of our 'whole selves' to 'Our' Father, not by loving him, but by loving one another with the love of the divine community."[1]

Not only does prayer presuppose community, promote and express it, but community, in its turn, results from prayer, presupposes prayer and makes it possible. It has already been suggested that the *agape* or love unifying true community is a gift of God and so must be prepared for by prayer. It is also true that praying together helps to strengthen this love by allowing it to be expressed in the presence of God. For prayer together allows the members of a community to express their real concern in Christ for one another, their desire that each person grow in Christ and become the person that the Father's love is calling him to be. Prayer, then, allows persons to be for each other in a new way and so provides a deepening dimension to community.

As part of this deepening dimension, prayer is presupposed in any true experience of community. This has already been suggested in terms of shared prayer, but it is equally true of any form of prayer, even the most hidden and "individual." Just as Christ prayed "That all be one," so too, a community, both in its expression of togetherness and in the "unspeakable groanings" of its individual members, must beg for the gift of true unity. Out of the individual's effort to meet God comes new strength and resolve to meet his brother. Out of the community's attempts to be for and with each other comes a real need to pray together.

So community leads to renewed prayer, to shared prayer. For a community that has begun to share human concerns soon transcends these and desires to share its need for creative relationship with God. This need to pray together is both an experience of human poverty, and also, an expression of human riches. The man who wants to be one with his brothers, who truly aches that this be accomplished in him, turns almost instinctively to praying with and for his brothers. With the strength of his brothers he finds his own prayer grows strong; with his brothers he can also face the poverty of his own resources for living in community; praying for his brothers allows him to remain in peace when his own poverty is almost overwhelmed by the obvious and overwhelming need of these same brothers. At the same time, these very real needs keep his own prayer honest. To pray that a brother will be comforted and then to deny him the courtesy of listening betrays one's own lack of true prayer. Similarly, the community can help a man to learn that his prayer has outreached his reality. For instance, to pray in the words of Paul, "That I may dissolve and be with Christ," when one has not lived and labored with the intensity of Paul is to be deceived. The day-to-day realism of community helps to uncover such dishonesty in prayer; the loving acceptance of community helps a man to keep his prayer focused on real need, in himself and in others.

The revelation of human need in community leads to prayer. It is also true that joy and new life develop a desire to celebrate community in prayer. Whenever we discover something good, we instinctively want to share it. Similarly a man who has come to love his brothers and has experienced something of the joy of mutual support and strength wants to consecrate this by giving thanks for it. So the gift of *agape* in community overflows very naturally into shared prayer. I want to thank my brother for who he is, and this is to thank the God who makes him be and become. I want to deepen my joy in the beauty of another person by praising all those who have given him life.

True community, then, makes prayer possible. Its joy and peace provide the quiet that prepares the way for openness and attentiveness to God. Discovering the beauty and goodness of other persons softens the heart and speaks realistically of a loving Father who waits for the opportunity of deepening prayer in order to give himself. Finally, the warmth of community can sustain the man of prayer in his hours of darkness and aloneness, the love of brothers can help a man to bear the growing knowledge of his own sinfulness, that vision which seems so much a part of authentic prayer.

Finally, community makes an experience of revelation possible and provides some of the conditions that are a necessary part of the revelatory process. In his relationships in community a man reveals himself, speaks of the kind of man he is, learns to grow in acceptance of the truth about himself. He also learns, existentially, that true revelation is conditioned by "trust, love, shared experience, common concerns."[2] Out of this human experience in community, a man comes to know that God's revelation of himself to the individual in prayer and to the community in shared prayer is also conditioned by trust, love, common concern. When God is silent, as he often seems to be in our world and in our lives, this may be the consequence of our lack of real belief that he has anything to say to us, that he loves us enough to share himself with us, that his concern for us transcends any dreams projected by self-love. Similarly, God trusts man, cares enough to share human concerns, loves each man in the human community. What God reveals in prayer is himself. And "God is found only in community. There shall never be discovery of God except by those in Christian community. God comes only to community makers.[3]

Meaning of community prayer

There is a real sense in which all prayer is communitarian. This follows from the obvious fact that all prayer is personal, and persons are, and come to be, only in relation to other persons. The very creation of man was an expression of God's prayer for the world. After this summation of his creative activity God rested. This resting of God from his work has been traditionally expressed by man through the observance of sabbath prayer. If it is God's creative act that makes man his image and likeness, a person, so to, it is the creative interaction of men with each other and with God that helps persons to grow and become themselves. When this creative response takes on something of the note of quiet and grateful response, then men enter specifically into prayer, an activity which is deeply, personally, and essentially communitarian.

All this suggests that all of man's prayer is rooted in personal relationships and so is rooted in community. It does not suggest in any sense that all prayer must be praying together, or that it must always be shared prayer. But surely some of the inter-personal nature of prayer will need to be expressed in these ways. Why? Just to make real this communitarian nature of true prayer by allowing it to express itself. Similarly, something of the reality of community is expressed both in praying together and in shared prayer. Praying together, i.e. being with others physically, concretely, at a certain time and place, sharing the material unity of certain forms and words, is one aspect of communal prayer. True personalism will never ignore this incarnational need of man to give body to his sharing in praying, by praying together.

On the other hand, such embodiment of community prayer can come to substitute for and be confused with the deeper reality of shared prayer. The result is men coming together to pray and never really communicating. In the poignant complaint of one of the Hasidic Masters of prayer, "I thought this was a House of Prayer but I find it so filled with prayers that there is no room for prayer." By way of contrast, the validity of praying together can be tested against the reality of the community shared prayer. The truth of such shared prayer can be found in the growth in love which it expresses and makes possible.

Sharing in prayer, then, will be an expression of the presence of the community to God and to each other. It will be an experience of a community "sensitive to and aware of each other, saying who they are together; that they have common desires, common needs, a common hope."[4]

In contrast to that group prayer in which each person is trying to safeguard his own devotion by keeping away from the reality of other persons in the praying community, shared prayer is marked by a real awareness of others, of their needs, and a parallel awareness of oneself in relation to these others. In shared prayer one gives expression to the awareness that all are called by God as a community, invited to become a community together. We listen to God's word as it is expressed in all the richness and variety of persons in community. We respond to this word, as it is expressed concretely in *this* praying community, gathered before the Father at *this* time.

In summary, what is shared transcends the materiality of time, or of space, or of words. What is truly shared is the reality of prayer itself. Thomas Clarke has described persons of prayer as people who are able to respond to values, rather than just react to situations.[5] In shared prayer persons gather together in order to share and to deepen their response, to assume responsibility in community for what affects the community of man, of church, of family, or of religious congregation.

Response to values is always a matter of community, since the creation of values is always communal. For example, I value something in terms of the value placed on it by others; my own evaluation is subjective, dependent on the valuing of other subjects. Even when I retain a value against the contrary estimate of others, my evaluation is still communitarian since it is a holding out against the community, and such opposition has enabled me to come to a deeper valuing of my own. In a similar way, the values expressed in the shared prayer of the community become my own values, not only in terms of the human psychology by which value systems are created but also through the action of the Spirit who speaks through the tongues of other persons in the community. In this same process, my own unique set of values becomes clearer, stands out against the values expressed in the prayer of other community members. In other words, individual charisms, as well as the charisms of the community, are strengthened in the expression of shared values of prayer.

Since individuals in community differ most precisely in those areas which are most personal to them, it follows that communities will also differ in what is most personal, their prayer expression. These very differences of one community from another will give further expression to the unique charism of each congregation. For at the heart of shared prayer is this community's expression of its own identity before God. How a community prays will say much about what it is for, how it reflects on its own service, what it values.

This shared prayer of a community must be related to life, and it must be honest and spontaneous. It must be related to the life of the praying community and not to the life of some idealized community. Authentic prayer will speak of the immediate problems of this community, its fears, its hopes. It will be an honest expression of these, erring on the side of bluntness, rather than risking the mask of artificiality and conventional phrasing. Finally, such prayer will be spontaneous, coming from the heart in freedom. Such honest, spontaneous prayer may be somewhat shy and embarrassed; it may be halting and ungrammatical. But it will be free in its expression and form.

This is not to say that shared prayer will be easy, but it will certainly not be complacent. To share is always somewhat hard for man, born into selfishness. And to share what is most precious comes even harder. So shared prayer will take time before prayer wells up out of the group and spills over into free expression. It takes patience with one's own fumbling efforts, the unfreedom of self and others. It takes faith: that man can pray, that this community of sinners can be converted to God this day, in this set of circumstances. The faith of a praying community will be surely tried, strained by the weakness, not only of its individual members but of the compounded weakness of the total group. If only the praying community, like the individual at prayer, can learn to believe and to wait, God himself will pray in this community. He has promised it, "Where two or three are gathered in my name. . . ."

Augustine wrote, "Better to go slow on the right road, than fast on the wrong one." Shared prayer is a right road but it is not a short-cut. Like growth in community itself, growth in shared prayer comes slowly, organically. It cannot be hurried if it is to remain true and free. It can only be appreciated as worth waiting for.

The practice of shared prayer

Application can now be made of the above to the specific practice of praying in community. Praying together in community can take the more formalized expressions of Mass, Sacraments and Office, or it can remain almost structureless to allow for maximum spontaneity. The more formalized structure of liturgical prayer allows a specific local praying community to incorporate itself, even in the form of its prayer expression, into the wider community of the whole praying church. But such prayer obviously lacks something of the realism and freedom of the more spontaneous prayer forms. It would seem that each of these expressions has some advantages and some disadvantages. Consequently some balance of both will be made for a better rounded prayer expression of the community. Actually, each individual community, like each member of that community, finds its truest expression in its own combination of liturgical prayer and spontaneous prayer. And each of these two forms, in itself, will also contain something of the other, so that liturgical prayer, today, has elements of true spontaneity, while spontaneous prayer must also be achieved in and tested against the more traditional forms of authentic Christian prayer.

Liturgical prayer is always shared prayer, a theological insight expressed in the use of plural pronouns in the prayers of the Eucharist and the celebration of the Sacraments. No Christian community, however, can be built up unless it has its basis and center in the celebration of the most holy Eucharist. Here, therefore, "all education in the spirit of community must originate."[6]

The liturgy, then, both expresses community and also helps to educate for it. When a community does not know itself, it cannot express itself, and consequently its liturgy will be poor and fumbling. The temptation, at this time, will be for individuals to seek out some liturgy that they, personally, will find meaningful, and so escape from the pain. But they will also escape from the challenge of forming true community and truly expressive liturgy. In this sense a fumbling liturgy, one that is stiff and somewhat awkward, may be more honest than a liturgy full of gimmicks and artificial togetherness. This is not to excuse poor liturgy in the name of poor community but only to indicate that these two realities are so interwoven they can only be improved together. It also indicates that a community that faces its liturgical poverty and seeks to grow liturgically as a community is on the way to truth.

A community that is seeking to discover itself in and through the liturgy will find that the prescribed prayers of the liturgy will become more and more its own prayers, that together the community will want to share in the total praise of the praying church. The community will also want to express its own unique reality at other parts of the liturgy. Similarly, participation in the Sacraments and the Office will be both universalized and particularized.

Since recent liturgical reforms have made clearer the essential outlines of the Eucharist and have already provided for both forms of communal prayer, it may be helpful to illustrate this blend of the formalized and the spontaneous in terms of the Office. Some praying together, as a group, of the traditional psalms and canticles will allow a specific local community to make contact with the rich prayer life of the past. The inclusion of specific readings, either from Scripture or from contemporary sources, will allow the individual community to pray together. Provision for periods of silence as part of the Office will also allow the community to reflect on what the Spirit has said and is still saying to the whole church and to this individual community. These reflections can then be shared as part of a community's attempt to do something more than *say* the Office.

Such shared reflection on the Scripture or some contemporary reading, either in the context of the Mass or as part of the shared prayer of the Office, provides one of the truest expressions of shared prayer. It has the benefit of being rooted and stabilized in the authentic tradition of the praying church, listening together to the word of God and responding together to his word. Such sharing of personal insights is not a discussion; rather it is a creative listening to and speaking out of God's word; it is God-centered, rather than man-oriented.

Today many persons are expressing interest in such shared prayer, either as rooted in response to Scripture, or as completely spontaneous and unstructured even in regard to topic. It is rather obvious that such prayer requires small groups, but what is less frequently indicated is the advantage of retaining the same persons in the group. This allows for a continuity of prayer and so lessens the kind of forced confession that sometimes threatens to turn spontaneous prayer into forced invasion of privacy. Another suggestion for groups seeking development in shared prayer is that of allowing and encouraging expressions of poverty and need. Such expressions seem best able to unite the group in communal openness, to keep the members honest and also to relax the tension of those who are less familiar with some of the newer prayer forms and feel threatened by what is still strange. Gradually, such shared prayer can provide one of the most realistic schools of prayer. For helping others to pray is less a matter of formal instruction and much more teacher-disciple relationship. Here the group becomes teacher and, at the same time, each member also retains something of the attitude of the disciple, always learning from the Spirit who speaks in the community.

In this spontaneous prayer of the group there is an opportunity to pray to Christ for the community and also to pray to Christ in the community. On the one hand, individuals may share their concerns for the needs of the community and help to make these needs truly communal. On the other hand, individuals can pray to the Christ who is in the community, expressing need for support and allowing individuals in the community to be specifically supportive;

they may ask for forgiveness from the community and in so doing prepare themselves to receive the forgiveness of Christ.

In the continuity of its group, its shared concerns, its life together which allows for deep understanding beyond the need for many words or explanations, the religious community is a privileged place for experimentation with the liturgy and with shared spontaneous prayer. As part of this experimentation in religious communities there seems special need to rediscover in the context of community, such time-honored realities as silence and solitude. In the past, silence tended to be equated with certain times, clock hours, when unnecessary noise and talking was forbidden. Unfortunately these times of silence were often empty times, periods of being cut off; they were anything but free periods, nor were they freeing. Consequently, periods of silence could not be shared, since these hours were somehow lacking in any meaning that could be shared. In contrast, silence that is filled with presence, that is an opening to something deeper, allows for a sharing that goes beyond words. Shared silence will often take on some concrete expression of respect for the silent periods of others, and hence, this provision for silence time will be a consequence of true interior silence rather than an imposition from without.

In a similiar way, deepening of shared prayer will, paradoxically, lead to growth in solitude. Dietrich Bonhoeffer in *Life Together* has warned, "Let him who cannot be alone, beware of community. Let him who is not in community beware of being alone."[7] This is to suggest that the mutual bond of prayer and community can also be expressed in the inter-relationship between solitude and community.

"Aloneness," it has been said, "as respect for another's solitude is a precious gift of community. Aloneness, when we should be supported by a brother, is loneliness." True community provides sufficient support so that each member can risk solitude without being lonely. In fact true solitude grows out of community and contributes to shared prayer. And it is one of the interesting developments, one of the criteria of authentic community and shared communal prayer, that it does lead to such solitude and deepening of the individual's personal contact with God in prayer.

Finally, this whole chapter on the inter-relationship of prayer and community, the meaning of shared prayer, and something on its practice can be summarized in terms of its new directions in the words of Thomas Clarke:

> Today we need to see that the journey of faith in the dark night is not only a plunge into the mystery of God but a descent into our humanity, a willingness to be human among humans (i.e. in community). It is here, I think, that we modern Christians are called to give a distinctly new expression to the imitation of Christ, to discipleship. This would imply a saying "yes" a willingness to let both God and man shape our destiny. It would also imply a standing up to adversity by what we may best call vulnerability—an availability for the other—for the Father and for men—that perseveres in the midst of adversity.[8].

So communal prayer is both a "Yes" and a "No"; it is both joy and pain. It is tremendously human, and yet faithful to the divine. It is like man, both immanent and transcendent; anchored in the reality of human community and, by means of this, open to communion with God.

SOME OF THE most critical questions being raised in the contemporary church are the survival questions that religious and religious congregations are asking themselves. Will religious life continue to exist in the church? Will future forms be recognizable? Will present forms evolve into these new types of religious life, or will presently existing congregations have to die out so that new communities can be founded? Specifically each religious congregation must ask these questions in terms of its own survival, its own unique charism: the young who will enter, the middle-aged who may or may not remain, the old who are dependent on the thinning resources of the congregation. Finally, individual religious agonize over their own vocational response. Some ask: Is this the same congregation which I entered twenty-five, or thirty, or forty years ago? Or is this community so different that I can no longer identify myself with it? Is my community degenerating into a crowd, or is it a group of persons who are on their way to becoming a full and total community?

All of these questions are caught up in an inquiry about the

charisms of a community. To be charismatic is to be gifted and
to be gifted for the other. In short, charismatic gifts are always
ways of serving others, ways of getting involved, of staying involved.
By your fruits you shall know them.

But not everything that looks like fruit is edible; which raises
the question of discernment of spirits. In no period of recent
history has this gift of discernment been so much needed. In the
past, rather clear guidelines attempted to spell out what was to be
considered good; past experience of fruitfulness was an adequate
criterion and, finally, authorities in church and in professional
fields could describe *safe* ways of proceeding. But today, criteria
out of the past are less and less applicable; experience quickly
loses touch with what exists here and now; and courageous trust
is needed to plan for a future that need never be. The agony of
repeated questioning of even the basic assumptions of religious life,
leaves many with precious little ground to stand on. Such exposure
is dangerous. It is also strengthening, rather like a small tree that is
constantly pulled and tugged by the rain and storm, and which
must rely on putting down deeper roots if it is ever to survive.

Part of this putting down of deeper roots might well be the
discovery of ever more appropriate ways to discern spirits and to
recognize the good fruits of true growth. The following pages will
describe some criteria for discernment, and then attempt to describe
some of the fruits of true growth in community.

Discernment of spirits

Growth in community can be identified as one of the clearest
signs of the working of the Spirit in our times. Whether it is the
chilling awareness that men today will either grow together or
die in separateness, it is still one of the graces of our times that
we increasingly realize that community is not a luxury for the few
but a necessity for all. Today no man can afford to ask, "Am I
my brother's keeper?" with any note of doubt, much less denial. To

refuse such responsibility is to act irresponsibly. It is to risk disillusionment and ultimate death. On the other side of the coin, never before has mankind had such opportunities for contacting his brother, for sharing his knowledge, for furthering the growth of all men. When such coming together happens, there is a kind of pre-evangelization that prepares for the good news of unity in Christ our brother, and God our father. Anything that brings persons together in shared truth, in enriched experience, in mutual help is indicative of the working of the Spirit.

Anything that introduces separation, division, disunity, that threatens to fracture the unity of community, has something of suspicion about it. But this is not to say that every natural affinity is beyond any further examination. For something that introduces a certain amount of confusion may be a necessary part of growth toward still greater unity. So discernment in this case, as ultimately in every case, calls for patience. It is not just a question of "How does this appear?" but rather a consideration of "Where does this lead?" If one answers that it leads to unity, then it is redemptive, which implies that it is both a kind of dying and a rising.

A second indication of the action of the Spirit, according to Ladislas Orsy, is an element of unexpectedness.[1] Again, this is not to suggest that everything that is unexpected is of the Spirit, but only to point out that what is of the Spirit will often be unexpected. This surely follows from the nature of the Spirit of truth, who is also the Spirit of freedom, a Spirit who blows where he wills. Another characteristic suggested by Father Orsy is that of humanity, the capacity to incorporate a certain grace that fits into the "human-ness" of the individual and of the community. In short, the gifts of the Spirit do not destroy a man or community. Rather they take the good that is there and make it holy and still more beautiful, more integral. The gifts of the Spirit are always gifts of growth from within and not additions by accretion.

Finally, the gifts of the Spirit have a certain blend of abundance on the one hand, and practicality on the other. The abundance of the Spirit says much about the *size* of God, how great and good and generous he is, beyond any human expectation. What he gives is never just enough; it is always expressed in the overflowing generosity of the miracle of the loaves and the fishes. If abundance is one of the signs of God's action, practicality is another. God's gift is not just an external help but an internal process of growth and interior development. It is for action and expresses itself in concrete ways. Every charism is given for others, but it also affects the life and practices of the one who receives it. It is a gift of expressing in life what one believes, of discovering how little one can do by oneself. It is a gift of admitted poverty, of receptivity, which makes holiness something beyond purely human effort. Which is to say again that it is a gift of acknowledged need of community.

Fruits of the Spirit

Granted that discernment of the Spirit has a certain communitarian orientation insofar as it is characterized by increasing unity, an unexpectedness, a certain integral humanness, and an abundance coupled with practicality, it follows that the fruits of the growing acceptance of the action of the Spirit will also be marked by such person-oriented characteristics as: ability to respond, willingness to be a disciple at any cost, increased desire for prayer, true freedom, a spirit of truth, growth in collegiality, in acceptance of pluralism and, finally, a note of strong hopefulness. When there is evidence of such growth in community, there is also strong reason for believing that the Spirit of holiness and love is active.

When a community is growing toward greater unity in the Spirit, it will be marked by an increased sense of personal and community responsibility. As has been suggested before, this will include a greater ability to substitute response for simple reaction. The spirit of this world is the spirit of immediate reaction to surface appearances, growing out of one's own self-centered approach to life. While reaction is characterized by a certain heat and an accompanying strong pull of emotion, true response is accompanied by a growing sense of resolution and peace. It is also distinguished by an increased sense of responsibility for what one does, for what the community does.

Just as the responsible man is one who can answer, reflectively, for the why of his action, so too, the responsible community can answer for its own identity and purpose. Part of this responsibility, of both the individual and the community, will be evidenced in the ability of persons to go out of themselves to others. The selfish immature person tends to retreat more and more into isolation when he is confronted with difficulties and disappointments. In contrast, the maturing person finds himself growing in openness to others, their needs, desires, even unspoken hopes and fears. This going out of self to others is an essential part of asceticism; and the increasing ability of a community to serve ever widening circles of other communities is a comparable sign of growth.

Some of the most hopeful signs of renewal in religious communities center around this capacity for responsible action. Individual members of community are experiencing an increasing need to answer for themselves, for their own commitment as religious, for their own lived expression of the evangelical counsels. Another evidence of this renewed responsibility is the awareness that individual religious must answer for not only their own renewal but also the renewal of their communities. Change in communities will come when the members work for and direct change; conversion will come when the members are converted. Similarly, individual members are coming to new awareness of their need to support each other. In more settled periods, rules and other structures provided some of this stability and support; today it must come primarily from the strength of community concern. When this concern is lacking, community is weakened, and everyone in the community must accept some responsibility for this weakness. The *how* of such support is itself a matter of constant conversion, for support which suffocates is obviously not strengthening; in contrast, support that enables a group to share in truth, to grow in love, is marked by the action of the Spirit's gift of himself.

One of the clearest signs of the Spirit's gifts in a community is the growing experience of deepening peace. Not a peace that speaks more of good health, or happy disposition, or pleasant experience, but a peace that endures despite difficulties, fatigue, criticism and even in the face of rejection. Such an experience of quiet acceptance and grateful openness goes beyond anything that the feelings of a man can summon out of his own resources; it can only be the gift of the Spirit, a Spirit who goes beyond man. This is the peace that allows for growing commitment in the face of crisis, deepening prayer in times of darkness, and renewed desire to serve in the face of rejection: It is a peace that remains faithful despite fears, that develops inner sureness despite questioning, that grows through and in the face of real diminishments. In short this is peace that allows the pain of passion to point toward the promise of resurrection.

This brings us to a third fruit of the Spirit: a willingness to pay the cost of discipleship. To be a disciple of any man, under any set of conditions, involves a kind of dying, since it means an opening of self, a letting go, a willingness to be taught, a desire to follow that goes even deeper than that most human instinct of *my* way, in *my* time, for *myself*. To be a disciple of a God who can ask anything because he is God is to let go of all human securities in the deeper security of total trust. But this is such a radical opening to death-in-promise-of-life that it is possible only in the support, strength, and discernment of others. This is particularly true in those periods when the "dying" is more in evidence than any beginning realization of new life. It is at these moments that human warmth, at least the realization that one has been known and loved truly by another human person, makes possible a more vital opening to the action of God's love.

But such discernment of the Spirit, acting in one's periods of darkness and difficulty, is only possible in the context of deepening prayer. The capacity for such prayer is still another sign and fruit of communion and community. As has already been suggested in the preceeding chapter, prayer and community are so inter-related that the deepening of one is always growth in the other. So the capacity to pray, "Lord, that I may see," and to mean it, is always an invitation to grow in realization of oneself in relation to a community. It is a risk to pray with such openness: a risk that one may discover unexpected ways of serving, new obligations of moving away from selfish interests to self-gift. Such prayer, when it is sincere, also reveals that no man has a right to judge another man; all stand before a God who judges. It is an opening of oneself to this God who tests every man by the communitarian standard of "What you do to the least of my brothers, you do to me."

Another criterion of growth in the Spirit and accompanying growth in community is a greater sense of freedom. For the Spirit of the Lord is always a Spirit of freedom, and a Christian can always be identified as a free man. If this identification seems a new concept, it is actually as old as St Paul, as communitarian as the work of the Spirit in the early church. Such freedom is the result of free choices, but free choices are possible only when a man can be himself. Since the finding of self and the losing of what is not really oneself is only possible in communion with others, it follows that growth in freedom is a fruit of true com-munity. Only men who freely desire community can enter into community, and only a free community can form such men. Such a free and freeing community results from the liberating commit-ment of persons with each other and to Christ.

One aspect of growing freedom is a capacity for truth. This fruit of community is evidenced by an ability to discern what is true and to respond to it with living acceptance. Truth, like freedom itself, does not always come in clearly marked packages; often it is hidden in obscure desires and awkwardly phrased re-quests; it comes through in hard-to-take criticisms and sharp-edged reproaches. Truth hides in the words and actions of unlikely people. But community gives privileged access to truth: the trust of living together, the honesty of real friends; the discernment of many different people, each of whom sees things, as no other ever sees, or ever will see them. In community, the truth that is connatural to certain cultures, certain persons, certain ages and stages of development can come through for the mutual enrichment of all. For example, the vision of the young can be tempered by the patience of the old, while the fears of the old melt before the enthusiasm of the young. The prophet who sees the one truth so clearly that he risks losing the surrounding area of grey in which most people must live can be supported and, at the same time, tempered in community. The man who knows far more truth than he can live can still be encouraged to share his discoveries and be supported to bear his own weakness. Growing ability of the strong to temper their truth, of the weak to speak out clearly what they see, both are fruits of growing community; both are a renewed preparation for that eternal and perfect community where every man will know as he is known, and love as he is loved.

Another fruit of community, another sign of growth, is the capacity of a group to live together, in true collegiality and a realistic practice of subsidiarity. Both of these principles become operative only in the light of honest belief in persons. To share authority, as collegiality implies, is to live in mutual respect and truth. It is to allow each man to be responsible for himself, for the community. It is to entrust oneself to another. In practice his spirit of collegial sharing permits another man to exercise positions of *authority*; those who have in the immediate past authorized the decisions will now have to let go. On the other hand, the persons who now receive a share in auhority must take up their responsibility.

It is only too tempting to circumvent this difficult asceticism of collegiality and accompanying subsidiarity. The person in a position of authority will be tempted to delegate the execution of certain areas of work while retaining the responsibility for these concerns. In this way, he obtains the benefits of delegation without paying the price of sharing. In a somewhat similar process, the person who is in the subsidiary position can take to himself the power of freedom in execution, the pleasure of praise, while refusing the responsibility of answering for consequences, of living with blame. In a truly collegial community there is a sharing of both authority and responsibility, an honest handing over of both work and concern. Because the implementation of subsidiarity involves so much asceticism of truth, so much realism of love, these are some of the most authentic indicators of growth in the community and in the Spirit.

One final suggestion of a fruit of community is a development of the courage and joy that are born of hope. Without hope, a man is lost; in hope he is saved. The Constitution on the Church in the Modern World speaks of "the strength which comes from hope" (no. 22). It might also have pointed to the debilitation which follows from a feeling of hopelessness. Granted that despair and anguish are signs of our time, where does the Christian find hope? It seems that he must begin his search in the human community. With other men and through their efforts, he needs to experience that man is redeemable and also redeemed. He needs to know that the pledge of consecration in virginity has meaning in a hoped for and yet distant future. He must see in persons who are willing to share all they are and have, a promise that poverty can be an opening to the riches of God. He needs to experience that the search for God's will in a community of brothers is already a pledge of unity in truth and love.

In the joy of a community, a man comes to experience that he can grow and become, that his past mistakes are forgotten, that his present fears are supportable, that his despair of a future can be relieved by the promise of other men. This is the human hope of what men can do together, what they can become in the strength of their love. It is also an experience which makes possible faith and hope in full life in the future, where all men will be one in themselves, with each other, in community and in communion. So human community is always a beginning; it is a promise of and a call to transcendence. "Bear with one another charitably, in complete selflessness, gentleness and patience. Do all you can to preserve the unity of the Spirit by the peace that binds you together. There is one Body, one Spirit, just as you were all called into one and the same hope when you were called. There is one Lord, one faith, one baptism and one God who is Father of all, over all, through all and within all" (Eph 4:2-6).

Notes

NOTES FOR CHAPTER TWO

1. Ernst Ranly, *Scheler's Phenomenology of Community* (The Hague: Martinus Nijhoff, 1966), p. 67.
2. *Ibid.*, p. 56.
3. *Ibid.*, p. 68.
4. Reinhold Niebuhr, *Man's Nature and his Communities* (New York: Scribner's, 1965), pp. 108–109.
5. Martin G. Plattel, *Social Philosophy* (Pittsburgh: Duquesne University Press, 1965), pp. 87–88.
6. Pierre Teillhard de Chardin, *The Appearance of Man* (New York: Harper & Row, 1965), p. 256.

NOTES FOR CHAPTER THREE

1. Dietrich Bonhoeffer, *Life Together* (New York: Harper & Brothers, 1954), p. 21.
2. Anthony Padovano, "The Problem of God," *Ave Maria* 105 (February 11, 1967), 18.
3. Bonhoeffer, *op. cit.*, p. 21.
4. *Ibid.*, pp. 23–24.

5. *Ibid.*, pp. 25–26.
6: *Ibid.*, p. 30.

NOTES FOR CHAPTER FOUR

1. Cf., Adrian Van Kaam, *Personality Fulfillment in Religious Life* (Pittsburgh: Duquesne University Press, 1967), pp. 157–162.
2. *Ibid.*, pp. 152–153.
3. Gabriel Moran, *Experiences in Community* (New York: Herder and Herder, 1968), p. 21.
4. Eugene Kennedy, *Fashion Me a People* (New York: Sheed & Ward, 1968), p. 150.
5. Moran, *op. cit.*, p. 99.

NOTES FOR CHAPTER FIVE

1. Cf., Gabriel Moran, *Experiences in Community* (New York: Herder and Herder, 1968), p. 10,
2. *Ibid.*, p. 201.
3. Rosemary Reuther, "Schism of Consciousness," *Commonweal* 87 (May 31, 1969), 327.
4. John Heijke, *An Ecumenical Light in Religious Community Renewal* (Pittsburgh: Duquesne University Press, 1966), p. 100.

NOTES FOR CHAPTER SIX

1. Robert Johann, *Building the Human* (New York: Herder and Herder, 1968), p. 64.
2. Pierre Teilhard de Chardin, *The Future of Man* (New York: Harper & Row, 1964), pp. 11–12.
3. Patrick Granfield, "Interview with Yves Congar," *America* 111 (May 6, 1967), 677.
4. Cf., Harvey Cox, *The Secular City* (New York: Macmillan, 1965), pp. 121–122.
5. Johann, *op. cit.*, p. 64.
6. Sister Marie Raymond and Morris I. Berkowitz, "Change in Institutional Symbolism: The Responses of Sisters to a Modification of Habit," *Review for Religious* 26 (1967), 295.
7. Jeremiah Newman, *Change and the Catholic Church* (Baltimore: Helicon, 1965), p. 24.

8. Abbé Houtart, *Challenge to Change* (New York: Sheed & Ward, 1964), p. 81.

9. Roger Schutz, *Dynamique du Provisoire* (Taizé: Les Presses de Taizé, 1965), p. 95.

10. Heijke, *op. cit.*, pp. 100–101.

11. Sister Charles Borromeo Muckenhirn, "A Theologian Looks at the American Sister Today and Tomorrow," *Conference of Major Superiors of Religious Women* (Washington, 1965), 126–127.

12. Houtart, *op. cit.*, p. 90.

13. Meriol Trevor, *Newman: Light in Winter* (New York: Doubleday, 1963), p. 528.

NOTES FOR CHAPTER SEVEN

1. Vincent Branick, "Formation and Task," *Review for Religious* 28 (January, 1969), 13.

2. *Ibid.*, 15.

3. *Ibid.*, 14–15.

4. Eugene Kennedy, *Fashion Me a People* (New York: Sheed & Ward, 1968), p. 152.

5. Eugene Kennedy, *Comfort My People* (New York: Sheed & Ward, 1968), p. 205.

6. Branick, *art.* cit., 16.

7. Gabriel Moran, *Experiences in Community* (New York: Herder and Herder, 1968), p. 36.

NOTE FOR CHAPTER EIGHT

1. Margery Williams, *Velveteen Rabbit* (Garden City: Doubleday and Co., n.d.), p. 17.

NOTES FOR CHAPTER NINE

1. Karl Rahner, "Asceticism," in *Theological Dictionary* (New York: Herder and Herder, 1965), p. 38.

2. Pierre Teilhard de Chardin, *The Divine Milieu* (New York: Harper & Row, 1965), p. 96.

3. *Ibid.*, p. 101.

4. Bernard Haring, "Asceticism in Religious Life," *Sister Formation Bulletin* 12 (1966), 27.

5. Donald Lehman and John Corrigan, "Self-Denial," *America* 112 (March 20, 1966), 393.

6. (Taizé: Presses de Taizé, 1965), pp. 11–12.

7. *Art. cit.*, 14.

8. Teilhard de Chardin, *op. cit.*, p. 100.

9. Eugene Kennedy, *Comfort My People* (New York: Sheed & Ward, 1968), p. 100.

10. Hans Urs von Balthasar, "A Theology of the Evangelical Counsels," *Cross Currents* 16 (Winter, 1966), 216.

11. Harvey Cox, *The Secular City* (New York: Macmillan, 1965), p. 230.

NOTES FOR CHAPTER TEN

1. Reinhold Niebuhr, *Man's Nature and His Communities* (New York: Scribner's, 1965), p. 84.

2. *Ibid.*

3. Sister Gregory Sheehy, "Enemies of Community," *Sisters Today* 40 (October, 1968), 110.

NOTES FOR CHAPTER ELEVEN

1. Gabriel Marcel, *Creative Fidelity* (New York: Farrar, Straus, 1964), p. 134.

2. Marcel, *Homo Viator* (New York: Harper & Row, 1962), p. 132.

3. *Ibid.*

4. Quentin Lauer, "Belief and Unbelief," *Cross Currents* 42 (Winter, 1967), 514.

5. *Ibid.*, 513.

6. James Carmody, "Contemporary Faith and Prayer," *Sisters Today* 39 (November, 1967), 100.

7. *Ibid.*, 102.

8. Peter A. Campbell and Edwin M. McMahon, *The In-Between: Evolution in Christian Faith* (New York: Sheed & Ward, 1969), p. 177.

9. Anthony Padovano, "The Problem of God," *Ave Maria* 105 (February 18, 1967) 18.

10. Donald Johnston, "Lonergan and the Redoing of Ethics," *Continuum* 5 (Summer, 1967), 216.

11. Lauer, *art cit.*, 515.

12. Carmody, *art. cit.*, 162.

NOTES FOR CHAPTER TWELVE

1. Peter A. Campbell and Edwin M. McMahon, *The In-Between: Evolution in Christian Faith* (New York: Sheed & Ward, 1969), p. 145.

2. Gabriel Moran, *Experiences in Community* (New York: Herder and Herder, 1969), p. 86.

3. Anthony Padovano, "The Problem of God, *Ave Maria* 105 (February 18, 1967), 17–18.

4. Sister Elaine Marie Prevallet, "Reflections on Prayer and Religious Renewal," *Review for Religious* 28 (July, 1969), 538.

5. Thomas Clarke, "Can Man Encounter God Today?" *Prayer* (Glen Rock, N.J.: Paulist Press, 1969), p. 17.

6. *Decree on the Ministry and Life of Priests*, no. 6.

7. Dietrich Bonhoeffer, *Life Together* (New York: Harper & Brothers 1954), p. 77.

8. Clarke, *art. cit.,* 15–16.

NOTE FOR EPILOGUE

1. Ladislas Orsy, "Charisms in Community," *Experimentation in Community* (Notre Dame, Ind.: University of Notre Dame Press, 1969).